THE NEW MERMAIDS

The Way of the World

THE NEW MERMAIDS

General Editor
BRIAN GIBBONS
Professor of English Literature, University of Münster

Previous general editors of the series have been:
PHILIP BROCKBANK
BRIAN MORRIS
ROMA GILL

The Way of the World

WILLIAM CONGREVE

Edited by
BRIAN GIBBONS
Professor of English Literature
University of Zürich

LONDON/A & C BLACK

NEW YORK/W W NORTON

Reprinted 1986, 1988, 1991, 1992
by A & C Black (Publishers) Limited
35 Bedford Row, London WC1R 4JH

First published in this form 1971
by Ernest Benn Limited

Published in the United States of America by
W. W. Norton & Company Inc.
500 Fifth Avenue, New York, N.Y. 10110

Printed in Great Britain
by Whitstable Litho Printers Ltd.,
Whitstable, Kent

British Library Cataloguing in Publication Data

Congreve, William, *b.1670*
   The way of the world.—(The New Mermaids).
   1. Title   2. Gibbons, Brian, *date*
   3. Series
   822'.4   PR3364.W3

ISBN 0-7136-2898-7
ISBN 0-393-90004-5 (U.S.A.)

CONTENTS

Acknowledgements	ix
Introduction	xi
The Author	xi
The Play	xvii
The Sources	xxxi
The Text	xxxiii
Further Reading	xxxv
THE WAY OF THE WORLD	1
Dedication	3
Prologue	7
Dramatis Personae	9
Text	11
Epilogue	115

ACKNOWLEDGEMENTS

AMONG MODERN editions of *The Way of the World* I have most frequently consulted those by Montague Summers, Kathleen Lynch, and Herbert Davis; I have referred to them occasionally in the commentary to the present edition by their editors' surnames. I owe much to the biographical study of Congreve by John C. Hodges (*William Congreve: Letters and Documents*) and something also to discussions at the symposium on Congreve held in September 1970 at the University of York.

The present edition has been prepared with the help of photocopies and books, for the use of which I have to thank the Directors of the British Museum and the Librarians of the University of Cambridge and the University of York. In conclusion I would like to thank the General Editors for their assistance.

York   BRIAN GIBBONS
June 1971

ACKNOWLEDGMENTS

INTRODUCTION

THE AUTHOR

WILLIAM CONGREVE was born in Yorkshire on 24 January 1670,[1] but spent his youth in Ireland, where his father served as a lieutenant in the English garrisons at Youghal and Carrickfergus, being transferred when Congreve was twelve to Kilkenny, where the boy was able to attend one of the best schools in the British Isles. From there in April 1686 Congreve went as a classical scholar to Trinity College, Dublin, then at a peak of intellectual and academic excellence. It is possible that Congreve's interest in the stage began, like Southerne's and Farquhar's, with visits to Dublin's Smock Alley Theatre;[2] but the Revolution of 1688 drove Congreve away to England, and he probably arrived in London about the middle of 1689, and entered the Middle Temple to read law in March 1691.[3]

Congreve soon gained the attention and affection of John Dryden, lately Poet Laureate and now sixty years old; his respect for Congreve's classical scholarship and creative talent resulted in the invitation to translate the eleventh satire in a collection of Juvenal published in 1692. In the same year Dryden published Congreve's commendatory verses as sole preface to his translation of Persius, Congreve himself brought out his short prose romance *Incognita*, and finally he showed the script of his first comedy, *The Old Bachelor*, to Dryden. With the recommendation of Dryden and Southerne it was acted at the Theatre Royal in 1693 with brilliant success. Congreve was twenty-three, and claimed to have written the play even earlier, presumably during his first year at the Middle Temple.[4] He dedicated it to Charles Boyle, whose Irish estates Congreve's father had begun to manage in 1690; the gesture is characteristic of Congreve in its combination of filial piety, judicious worldliness, and social grace.

[1] Biographical facts are taken from John C. Hodges, *William Congreve : Letters and Documents* (London, 1964).

[2] For an account of the Smock Alley Theatre see W. S. Clark, *The Early Irish Stage* (Oxford, 1955).   [3] Hodges, op. cit., p. 89.

[4] For discussion of this question see the present writer's 'Congreve's *The Old Bachelor* and Jonsonian Comedy' in *William Congreve*, Mermaid Critical Commentaries (London, 1972).

In the same year, 1693, his second comedy *The Double Dealer* had a disappointing reception at the Theatre Royal. Dryden lent powerful support by contributing a verse commendation published with the play, and Congreve, in the dedication, angrily refuted hostile criticism based, as he maintained, on misapprehension of the comic mode of the play. However, there is a weakness in its melodramatic portrayals of villainy and innocence which betrays the uncertainly controlled influence of the Jacobean dramatist John Fletcher, even though the play marks a key stage in Congreve's artistic development: it is his first attempt to develop a comic mode which can incorporate serious human experience without discarding the essential richness of the inherited comic tradition.

From this point of view, Congreve's next play, *Love for Love* (1695), appears to confirm his early gift for conventional gay comedy, rather than to present a further development of the mode of *The Double Dealer*. Yet *Love for Love* was a success, it gave Congreve fame and reputation, and amply rewarded Dryden for his faithful support of the young dramatist. Moreover, the play does certainly exhibit a new richness in characterisation, where frequent debts to Shakespeare, as well as Ben Jonson, are apparent.

In the same year, 1695, Congreve wrote the letter to Dennis concerning humour in comedy, which though not itself an important critical essay is a confirmation of the deep agreement in matters of principle between Dryden and Congreve, not merely as friends, but as creative artists. Congreve shared Dryden's convictions, especially in his emphasis on Ben Jonson as a model for comic writers, his admiration for the Roman playwright Terence, and his faith in the supreme genius of the English for comedy, while Dryden looked to the young Congreve to fulfil the ideal set forth in his essay *Of Dramatic Poesy*, that an English comic dramatist should learn from the genius in characterisation of Shakespeare, the correctness and strength in design of Jonson, the gaiety in spirit of Fletcher, and the polish and grace in dialogue of Dryden's own age. When Congreve, in dedicating *The Way of the World* to Montague, attributed the quality of its dialogue to his experience of the earl's conversation, the explicit compliment to Montague was also therefore an implicit homage to Dryden; in addition, Congreve probably recalled that Dryden had paid exactly the same compliment to the Earl of Rochester in the dedication of *Marriage à la Mode* in 1672.

Congreve, in the dedication to Montague, had compared his patronage to that which Scipio and Laelius afforded Terence. This is really much more than an agreeably civilised classical allusion; it is characteristic of Congreve's graceful and truly witty scholarship, for the comparison holds fully, and implies much about Congreve's attitude to his own career.

Terence,[5] who commanded the profound respect of Ben Jonson and of Dryden, is famous for his development of the Greek comedy of Menander, for the subtlety and elegance of his dialogue and characterisation, for his introduction of double-plots and complex romantic intrigues in place of the lively farcical manner of his predecessor Plautus, and for a career brief, brilliant, and controversial. Like Congreve, Terence wrote his first play at twenty-one; he read it to an elderly Roman dramatist, who admired it, and the play had a brilliant stage success. Terence won entry into the best social and intellectual circle in the capital, where he found defenders and patrons, but he suffered on occasion from the bad taste of audiences who, disappointed by the absence of farce in his *Hecyra*, turned away to the rival attractions of tightrope walkers, boxers, and gladiators. Congreve could find here obvious analogies to the taste which rejected *The Double Dealer* and preferred such crude comedies as *Love and a Bottle* to *The Way of the World*. Even more exact, moreover, was the parallel between Collier's attack on Congreve and the persecution of Terence by an old playwright Luscius Lanuvinus, who plagued him with accusations of having contaminated his Greek sources, and remained obstinately blind to Terence's true concern, the creation of a subtler comic mode which substituted complexity in character and situation for the caricature and farce of the preceding age.

Congreve had been grateful for the defence which his friend Dryden's authority had afforded, when *The Double Dealer* was attacked; but four years later, when Congreve became one of Jeremy Collier's targets in the notorious *A Short View of The Immorality and Profaneness of the English Stage*, he replied with his own *Amendments of Mr Collier's False and Imperfect Citations*, no doubt fully conscious of the ironic parallel between the Roman and Puritan English meanings of 'contamination'.[6]

In his *Amendments*, Congreve argues with a lawyer's skill and a dramatist's spontaneous wit and immediacy of effect. His performance begins by playfully reversing Collier's images of dirt on to

[5] Details of Terence's career are taken from W. Beare, *The Roman Stage* (London, 1964).

[6] Lanuvinus used 'contaminatio', apparently, in the sense of *spoil* not *soil* or *pollute*; he was arguing that Terence was not producing faithful versions of Greek comedy but, by using several plays as the basis for a single play of his own, he was spoiling his inheritance; Jeremy Collier, on the other hand, accused Congreve of polluting the English stage with profaneness and immorality.

Collier's own head. Collier becomes for Congreve 'the evil Spirit', the thing of darkness, who has 'blackned the Thoughts with his own *Smut*', and therefore, declares Congreve, 'for his *Foot pads*, which he calls us in his Preface, and for his *Buffoons* . . . I will onely call him Mr. *Collier*'.[7] The tone is sprightly here, though it later becomes indignant. It has been suggested that Collier's attack made an impression on Congreve which resulted in the greater seriousness of theme in *The Way of the World*. It is true that Congreve's defence of the hero of *Love for Love*, Valentine, against Collier, adopts a sobriety of tone and attitude which is not really appropriate to the atmosphere of the play; Congreve declares 'the Character is a mix'd Character; his Faults are fewer than his good Qualities; and, as the World goes, he may pass well enough for the best Character in a Comedy; where even the best must be shewn to have Faults, that the best Spectators may be warn'd not to think too well of themselves'.[8]

The comment is interesting, particularly the phrase 'as the World goes', for if it seems unsuited to *Love for Love* it certainly is appropriate for the comedy which Congreve was actually composing at the time, *The Way of the World*, which first appeared at Lincoln's Inn Fields Theatre the following March, 1700.

It is evident from the substance of Congreve's dedication of this last comedy that he considered it his masterpiece, while his tone seems valedictory, implying his state of mind after the disappointing public reception of the play. If he were to cease writing comedy now, at the age of thirty, he would leave a complete if small oeuvre; there was critical controversy about its value, but he was confident that it met the highest classical standards; and there was also something extraordinary and compelling about the detailed coincidence between his own career and his venerated predecessors, Terence and Ben Jonson. Each of them had forged a new comic form, meeting controversy and proudly defying it in declamatory prefaces and prologues, appealing to the authority of classical precept and example, and achieving great reputations in posterity. Congreve's classical temper and his extraordinary sensitivity to pattern must have been attracted by the idea of a retirement from comedy which would complete the parallel between himself, now thirty, and Terence, who left Rome at twenty-five after writing six comedies. Such an act, furthermore, would repeat the design of Ben Jonson's career, for he had been driven to temporary retirement after the

[7] Quotations from Congreve's *Amendments* are taken from Montague Summers, ed., *The Works of William Congreve* (London, 1923), III, 171–206.

[8] ibid., p. 200.

failure of *Catiline* by his contempt for the audience, and had proudly expressed his defiance in the *Ode to Himselfe:*[9]

> Come leave the loathed Stage,
> And the more loathsome Age,
> Where pride and impudence in faction knit,
> Usurpe the Chaire of wit:

Later in 1700 came the death of Dryden, and perhaps it was then that Congreve, with his extraordinary feeling for completed pattern, recognised in his own life the fulfilment of a design that rivalled art.

The relationship between Congreve's life and art seems to have been unusually and interestingly reciprocal, and we are not free to neglect Congreve's personal experience of the society of his time; dramatic comedy is, in any case, the most socially articulate form of the supremely social art of theatre, and there is point in weighing up the question. When Congreve came to London he was not rich. His favourable start was the result of his personal charm and his wit as much as his literary talent. He won entry to the select society of Dryden and the literary figures at Will's coffee house in Covent Garden, and this in turn led to entry into other circles: on one hand the society of the theatre, on the other of aristocrats like the Earl of Montague. Congreve's easy, graceful manners and gentlemanly tastes gained him the friendship and esteem of the famous and the great, but his career depended upon their influence and patronage, and he was obliged to handle his own modest means prudently and astutely for many years before he became at last rich. His early work displays an inclination to fantasy and absurdity, which give it great charm, but he was at the same time a student of law: his plays are plotted with strict and detailed precision, they deal with the manipulation of law to reconcile individual needs to social obligations, and they show the complex interweaving of relationships—of friendship, family, and business—in the select and intricate, polite metropolitan world.

In his personal affairs Congreve seems to have shown the judgement, tact, and humane good humour which characterise Mirabell himself. Dryden invited the legally knowledgeable Congreve to draw up his contracts with the publisher Jacob Tonson. The contract Congreve drew up for Dryden's *Virgil* was, it has been said, 'a shrewder document than one might expect from the poet';[10] evidently, however, Congreve matched legal acumen with tact.

---

[9] All quotations from Jonson taken from *Ben Jonson*, ed. C. H. Herford and P. and E. Simpson (Oxford, 1925–52).

[10] Hodges, op. cit., p. 76, points out that Congreve had been reading law for more than three years when this contract was drawn up.

He helped his friend Dryden, but his relationship with Tonson continued in later years to their mutual benefit, after Congreve had ceased to write and Dryden had died, for Tonson invited Congreve to join the Kit-Cat Club, founded about 1700 and including among its early members Steele, Walsh, Addison, Vanbrugh, and the Earl of Montague to whom Congreve had dedicated *The Way of the World*. Later, the Whig inclination of the Kit-Cat Club helped Congreve obtain the post of Secretary of Jamaica, and with prudent management of his lucrative salary Congreve amassed the fortune of ten thousand pounds.

This fortune became the focus of the memorable last act of his life. Congreve's attachment to Anne Bracegirdle had ceased, and in his last years he became the lover of the young Duchess of Marlborough. When her daughter Mary Godolphin was born in 1723 there was gossip that Congreve was the father, but most of this was forgotten when it developed that Congreve's will named the duchess' husband as executor, and it came to be accepted that the relationship had been platonic. In his will Congreve had first made the duchess executrix, then, no doubt with the aim of avoiding gossip or scandal, named her husband in her place. His true motives can only be understood by considering the interlocking will of the duchess, not written until four years later and not made public. Her will required that her body be buried not at Blenheim but in Westminster Abbey, near the Earl of Godolphin, that is, in the same part of the abbey as she had buried Congreve. Furthermore, her will dealt chiefly with her daughter Mary, to whom she specifically left 'all Mr Congreves Personal Estate that he left me', plate engraved 'with Mr Congreves Armes', three thousand pounds, and jewels worth seven thousand five hundred pounds purchased with the money Congreve left her. So, as John C. Hodges explains,[11]

> If Mary Godolphin was his daughter, he naturally wanted her to have his personal things, his plate engraved with the Congreve arms and the choice collection of books he valued so highly. And all this he wanted to pass along quietly, without scandal or embarrassment. He would hardly have considered naming Mary directly as his heir. To do so would multiply gossip without end. He could depend on the mother, as sole executrix, to care for his property and pass it along in her will to Mary. But on second thought, Congreve apparently realized that he could accomplish his purpose regarding his property and at the same time help to quiet gossip by naming the husband of the Duchess as his sole executor. The will, it should be noted, was carefully drawn to restrict the powers of the husband and to leave the Duchess entirely free to transmit Congreve's property (as she did) to Mary.

[11] ibid., p. 251.

Here Congreve achieved in his own life an 'artful solution of the fable', and contrived a plot which worked through the manipulation of law and the conveyance of an estate in trust, to achieve the essential resolution of comedy, 'an individual release which is also a social reconciliation'.[12]

THE PLAY

The titles of Congreve's successive comedies suggest a steady development and a concern with progressively wider areas of experience, beginning with the relatively limited scope of *The Old Bachelor* and concluding with that more comprehensive theme, *The Way of the World*. However, the maturity and range of Congreve's comedy are relative to the theatrical conditions which prevailed and to the actors who interpreted his roles, as well as to the strictly limiting conventions within which he wrote. Congreve practised a classical economy in stagecraft; he designed all his plots around the conventional set of comic roles, and accepted themes, of the comedy of manners; moreover, his four comedies were presented within a period of only seven years, at two theatres, the Theatre Royal and the Lincoln's Inn Fields Theatre, which differed only in the inferior size and condition of the latter.[13] *Love for Love*, in fact, had been 'read and accepted of at the Theatre Royal',[14] but Congreve withheld it during the dispute which led to Betterton's move to Lincoln's Inn Fields, where the play was then performed. In due course *The Mourning Bride* (Congreve's tragedy) and *The Way of the World* were performed there also.

This close continuity, which is so important an element in Congreve's plays, was further strengthened by the remarkably select number of actors who created the successive major roles. The same actor, Betterton, created Heartwell, Maskwell, Valentine, Osmyn, and Fainall; the same actress, Mrs Bracegirdle, created all Congreve's heroines from Araminta to Millamant; indeed only one major actor in *The Way of the World*, John Verbruggen, had not been in at least two of Congreve's previous comedies, and even he had once understudied Williams, the original Vainlove and Mellefont.

[12] Northrop Frye, 'The Argument of Comedy' in A. Nicoll, *The Theatre and Dramatic Theory* (London, 1962), p. 125.
[13] Cibber describes it at the time it was closed as 'but small, and poorly fitted up within the Walls of a Tennis *Quaree* Court, which is of the lesser sort': *An Apology for the Life of Mr Colley Cibber* (new ed. London, 1889), I,314–15.
[14] ibid., I, 197.

What is more, these were the most distinguished actors of the time: Betterton, the greatest Shakespearean actor between Burbage and Garrick; Mrs Barry, the most celebrated actress of the Restoration, famous for her tragic roles (Cibber:[15] 'In Scenes of Anger, Defiance, or Resentment, while she was impetuous and terrible, she pour'd out the Sentiment with an enchanting Harmony') but also the original Mrs Loveit in Etherege's masterpiece *The Man of Mode*. Having seen Mrs Barry's Lady Touchwood in *The Double Dealer*, Congreve doubtless had a compelling reason for his continuing pre-occupation with a more serious mode of comedy.

Among the comic roles a similar pattern is evident. Sir Wilfull was created by Underhill, a noted Gravedigger in *Hamlet*, and successful not only as Sir Sampson in *Love for Love* but in such buffoon roles as Justice Clodpate, Sir Nobel Clumsey, Lolpoop, Oldwit, and so on;[16] while Mrs Leigh, who created Lady Wishfort, had years before created the original of the part, Lady Woodvil in *The Man of Mode*. As for the heroine, Anne Bracegirdle, she was according to Cibber the darling of the theatre, and 'when she acted *Millamant* all the Faults, Follies, and Affectations of that agreeable Tyrant were venially melted down into so many Charms and Attractions of a conscious Beauty'.[17] It is said that Congreve was in love with Anne Bracegirdle, and Cibber retails the gossip that when Congreve gave her a lover in a play he seemed palpably to plead his own passion. Certainly the cumulative effect on the young dramatist of association with such gifted performers must have been richly rewarding, and for Congreve to see his plays interpreted by great actors must have been an educative experience, and no doubt contributed to the remarkable evolution of his art towards the mature assurance of his last comedy. It was his fortune to inherit a tradition which was supremely alive.

Congreve's talent for the creation of subtle characters and dialogue achieved full expression through actors of this high calibre; and in the stage conditions also his art found fulfilment. Here is Cibber again:

> the usual Station of the Actors, in almost every Scene, was advanc'd at least ten Foot nearer to the Audience than they now can be ... But when the Actors were in Possession of that forwarder Space to advance upon, the Voice was then more in the Centre of the House, so that the most distant Ear had scarce the least Doubt or Difficulty in hearing what fell from the weakest Utterance: All Objects were thus drawn nearer to the Sense; every painted Scene was stronger ... every rich or fine-coloured Habit had a more lively Lustre.[18]

[15] ibid., I, 160.   [16] ibid., I, 154–5.
[17] ibid., I, 173.   [18] ibid., II, 85.

The actors in this forward area played in front of painted flats
running in grooves within the proscenium arch and closing together
in the centre of the stage; if scenery or properties were needed
in the scene, these flats parted to disclose the inner stage.[19]

In *The Way of the World* all the action is designed to be played in
the forward area except for the initial discovery of Fainall and
Mirabell seated at cards in Act I, and for the perambulations in the
park in Act II, where both the forward and inner stages were probably used, with the park scene represented by painted flats, and
possibly also 'relieves', that is scenes in relief, moulded scenes, and
cut scenes where part of the flat was cut out to show a distant prospect
extending behind. For the rest, Congreve's requirements in painted
scenes were simple and formal: flats drawn across to represent the
room in Lady Wishfort's house, and the room in the chocolate-
house. Congreve's requirements may be seen as a conscious reflection
of the special sense of 'the world' when it means polite metropolitan
society with its rigid, formalised, and interchangeable façades,
limited in number, providing the flat background against which the
characters, so contrastingly full of animation, depth, and movement,
act in tension.

So, when the curtain draws for Act I, it discovers a conventional
theatrical tableau: two gamesters at cards in a chocolate-house. As
they rise and begin to converse, the card-game dissolves to become
a metaphor for the dramatic action, and the two men, at first sight so
similar, begin to acquire particular and very different identities.

The process is gradual; Congreve's exposition is indirect, much
of it conveyed by inference, for in this play it is at least as important
to establish the fluidity and uncertainty of the atmosphere as it is to
indicate the pattern of characters and plot. In the opening dialogue
there is a subtle instability of tone; the hints, evasions, and insinuations convey the impression of much being withheld; and precisely
this impression is necessary to a proper understanding of the play,
which is concerned to bring this intricate texture, the texture of real
life in society, into focus with the traditional ideals of comedy.
Congreve's purpose is to find a means of reconciling the ideals of
moral conduct with the actualities of social experience at the time;
in short, it is an endeavour to modify the art of comedy to make its
morality more inclusive and reconciliatory, less ideal and remote.

Congreve begins the play by emphasising the similarity between
the situation of Mirabell and that of Fainall, but as the action
develops it becomes clear that there is a crucial distinction between
them, and this is made explicit in the last scene when Mirabell,

---

[19] See Montague Summers, *The Restoration Theatre* (London, 1934).

having beaten Fainall at his own game, flings back at Fainall the cheap and base cynicism which has guided his embittered career in the play; for when Mirabell taunts him with the phrase 'the way of the world' [20] the audience will recall Fainall's use of it, first when reassuring his mistress Mrs Marwood that he loves her and would be rid of his wife, and has 'something of a constitution to bustle through the ways of wedlock and this world',[21] and the second time, when he learns of her adultery, he reflects bitterly that their doubly adulterous marriage is 'in the way of the world'.[22] Mirabell, however, lives differently, according to another interpretation of the phrase; and it is in Mirabell that Congreve exhibits his own ideal of virtuous action, something with which he was preoccupied at the time he wrote the play, to judge from his account of Valentine's career in *Love for Love*: 'he has honesty enough to close with a hard Bargain, rather than not pay his Debts, in the first *Act*; and he has Generosity and Sincerity enough, in the last *Act*, to sacrifice every thing to his Love; and when he is in danger of losing his Mistress, thinks every thing else of little worth'.[23] If we add to this the remark already quoted, that 'as the World goes, he may pass well enough for the best Character in a Comedy; where even the best must be shewn to have Faults, that the best Spectators may be warn'd not to think too well of themselves', Congreve's emphasis on Mirabell's prodigal past, and present dependence on the goodwill of Mrs Fainall, his ex-mistress, and Lady Wishfort, Millamant's aunt, becomes comprehensible. Underlying the comic action is the romantic theme of the hero proving his worth and winning the hand of the fair heroine; but the contrast between the situation of Mirabell and that of his Shakespearean ancestor Benedick is clear when we notice how complex and sophisticated – and prosaic – Mirabell's task is, where Benedick has but to challenge Claudio and refute Beatrice's charge that

> manhood is melted into curtsies, valour into compliment, and men are only turned into tongue, and trim ones too; (*Much Ado*, IV, i)

Benedick has courage, gaiety, hope untarnished by experience; such spirit informs the exchange between the lovers in *The Double Dealer* as Cynthia banters with Mellefont:[24]

> 'Tis an odd game we're going to play at: What think you of drawing Stakes

---

[20] V, 501.   [21] II, 188–9.   [22] III, 547.

[23] *Amendments*, ed.cit., III, 200.

[24] Quotations from other plays of Congreve taken from Herbert Davis, ed., *The Complete Plays of William Congreve* (Chicago and London, 1967).

Mellefont answers from the heart without denying his youthful inexperience; his response has hope, not wisdom, it has the strength that comes of immaturity:

> No, hang't, that's not endeavouring to Win, because it's possible we may lose; since we have Shuffled and Cutt, let's e'en turn up Trump now.   (II, 157–61)

With the opening of *The Way of the World*, imagery from cards offers itself as the natural way of describing the behaviour of Mirabell and Fainall, but the mood is very far from the gaiety of Mellefont and Cynthia, as each man seeks to elicit information from the other without revealing his own hand. The shifting texture of their conversation reflects their awareness of the complexity of the case, and if each man's motives become clearer as fragments of information emerge, there is still much that the audience does not know when the dialogue ends. The chief cause of tension between them is Mrs Marwood. She has frustrated the plan of Mirabell to gain Lady Wishfort's approval of his match with Millamant. Mirabell suspects Fainall of being Mrs Marwood's lover and privy to her designs; in his turn Fainall suspects her of being attracted to Mirabell (one reason why she frustrated the match, perhaps), so he seeks to establish whether Mirabell returns the sentiment or not.

When Fainall makes the jesting remark to Mirabell that he would not make love to a woman who undervalued the loss of her reputation, each of them at once thinks of the other's relationship to Mrs Marwood. Mirabell replies

> You have a taste extremely delicate, and are for refining on your pleasures.   (I, 10–11)

This is both an evasion of the proffered subject and a coolly ironic reproof of Fainall's libertine wit. Fainall counters by interpreting this reproof as merely a sign of ill-humour, and hints that he suspects the cause to be a woman. Mirabell denies it lightly, and Fainall reacts to the change in tone at once with his more bantering remarks about Millamant. Mirabell, instead of relaxing his guard, pursues this subject for some time, preserving the playful tone to fend off Fainall's leading questions and indirect insinuations without quite dropping the question of Mrs Marwood. Fainall becomes less oblique as his frustration increases, and much of his character is revealed in his choice of phrase:

> The discovery of your sham addresses to her, to conceal your love to her neice, has provoked this separation. Had you dissembled better, things might have continued in the state of nature.
>   (I, 59–62)

Mirabell neutralises the innuendo by resorting to playful nonsense about Lady Wishfort, then suddenly insinuates that Fainall is Mrs Marwood's lover. The quick reaction this provokes possibly suggests Fainall's guilt; certainly Mirabell's tone becomes more cool as he allows Fainall a glimpse of his private, contemptuous opinion of him:

> one of those coxcombs who are apt to interpret a woman's good manners to her prejudice

and then trumps Fainall's last bid:

FAINALL

> ... Yet you speak with an indifference which seems to be affected, and confesses you are conscious of a negligence.

MIRABELL

> You pursue the argument with a distrust that seems to be unaffected, and confesses you are conscious of a concern, for which the lady is more indebted to you than your wife.

(I, 85–90)

Mirabell fastidiously reorders Fainall's own phrases to make a penetrating judgement; Fainall does not reply, but makes a tactical withdrawal under the pressure of Mirabell's firm authority.

Now, it is sometimes argued that from a first reading of this conversation between Mirabell and Fainall, one might suppose there was no difference between the two men: that there is a tendency to coalescence in the dialogue.[25] This is unlikely to be a problem in the theatre, where actors will make provisional distinctions possible very early, but in any case a second encounter follows almost at once, and there the two men are clearly contrasted in their attitudes to love and marriage, in their feelings of generosity and cynicism. What is implicit, tentatively and subtly discernible, in the first encounter, becomes gradually explicit and clear. The initial obscurity is important, too: as the exposition unfolds in Acts I and II, the audience's understanding of Mirabell, and admiration for him, will evolve, but not without hesitations: 'even the best must be shewn to have Faults': and as a consequence Congreve's concern with conduct *in society* will come into clear focus.

In the dedication of *The Way of the World* Congreve wrote that his concern was with characters of affected wit: 'a wit, which at the same time that it is affected, is also false'. Fainall's falsity is deter-

[25] This point is made by Ian Donaldson, *The World Upside Down* (Oxford, 1970), p. 125. I cannot agree with him that Congreve's moral design in the play is insufficiently fastidious as a consequence of its narrative subtlety; rather I find the subtlety contributes to the moral fastidiousness of the design.

mined, forceful, and menacing later in the action, of course, but it is suggested with subtlety and consistency from the outset. So clear, indeed, is the logic of Congreve's exposition that details of the Mirabell-Fainall relationship not revealed until Act II help to explain, retrospectively, some of the tensions in the first conversation in the play. The essential distinction between Mirabell and Fainall – which must be a dominant concern – is in fidelity to genuine convictions, integrity, and generosity of feeling. Indeed, such is the superficial elegance and social awareness of Mirabell's discourse that it may be worth emphasising the strength and energy of his emotions; as Bonamy Dobrée[26] has well remarked, 'Not to see this passionate side of Congreve is to lose the best in him; it is like reading Shakespeare to find that he does not conform to classical rules'. Fainall's similarity to Mirabell is confined to the superficial facility in phrasing, the practised control of entertaining anecdote, malicious innuendo, and quickness in repartee, common to everyone in society, including, as Congreve takes pains to emphasise, such fools as Witwoud and Petulant.

This is not to say, of course, that there are not differences of degree among false wits in the play. On the contrary, there is a strict hierarchy, from Fainall – played by Betterton, and not a comic part – to Witwoud and thence to Petulant, who is nearly all vapour, and tends as a consequence to be explosive (so betraying his Elizabethan lineage).[27] This hierarchy of false wit is indicated by the order in which characters appear in Act I, so that the audience has the opportunity to measure each in turn against Mirabell, the true wit, and to compare relative degrees of folly. This gradual exposition is accompanied by successive moods, each more free than the last; in this way the transition is effected from the still tense mood of Fainall's second dialogue with Mirabell to the frankly farcical entrance of Petulant at the end of the Act.

The modulation from the opening mood to the freer comedy of Witwoud is effected in this second dialogue of Mirabell and Fainall, where Congreve succeeds in preserving the complex texture of their relationship while allowing the true spirit of comedy release. Fainall introduces once more the subject of Millamant, and, seeking to be both agreeable and amusing, remarks that she has wit. Mirabell's reply affects an even tone, but is full of feeling and warmth:

[26] *Restoration Comedy 1660–1720* (London, 1924), p. 146.
[27] There are echoes of Falstaff, Pistol, and even Corporal Nym in Petulant's speech—compare Petulant's threat of throat-cutting soon after his entrance in Act I with the similar threat of Nym (*Henry V*, II, i, 20–25, in *The Complete Works of Shakespeare*, ed. Peter Alexander (London, 1951)). Petulant is chiefly derived from Jonson's obstreperous fools, of course.

> She has beauty enough to make any man think so, and complaisance
> enough not to contradict him who shall tell her so.   (I, 137-8)

But Fainall has little taste for this, and deflects the conversation
back to repartee. Mirabell, whose feelings are now aroused, cannot be
diverted, and embarks on a fuller declaration of his love for Millamant and a fine expression of his generosity of spirit, which even
sweetens the potentially cynical figure of paradox:

> I like her with all her faults, nay, like her for her faults. (I,142-3)

Fainall responds with the curt, bitter, and revealing comment that
marriage changes all that:

> Ay, ay, I have experience: I have a wife, and so forth.   (I, 161)

The bitterness of Fainall is limiting and distorting, whereas the
warmth and generosity of Mirabell widen the range and enrich the
quality of his experience, and his speech.

Part of Mirabell's preoccupation, when conversing with Fainall,
is in gauging Fainall's relationship with Mrs Fainall. In Act I we
cannot know this, though we can detect Mirabell's implicitly reprov-
ing attitude to Fainall's cynical dismissal of his marriage. However,
Mirabell has good reason for concern at Fainall's evident alienation
from his wife, as the second Act reveals; and it is here that Congreve's
concern with a more inclusively realistic drama is apparent. The
scene between Mirabell and Mrs Fainall[28] is preceded by the passionate and painful encounter of Mrs Marwood and Fainall in which
accusations and counter-accusations, alternating with gestures of
defiance and conciliation, exhibit the essentially selfish quality of
their feelings and the corrosive effects of the liaison:

MRS. MARWOOD
> 'Tis false, you urged it with deliberate malice—'twas spoke in
> scorn, and I never will forgive it.

FAINALL
> Your guilt, not your resentment, begets your rage. If yet you
> loved, you could forgive a jealousy; but you are stung to find
> you are discovered.   (II, 158-62)

The contrast between this and the scene which immediately
follows between Mirabell and Mrs Fainall is deliberate, exact, and
significant. First we are shown Mrs Marwood with her partner in
adultery (Fainall); then Mrs Fainall with her erstwhile lover
(Mirabell). Although both men defend themselves by arguing that
they have preserved reputations,[29] they do so in contrasting ways

[28] II, 222-85.   [29] II, 173, 234.

which reveal much: Mirabell's admission is not evasive or aggressive, but gentle and reasonable as well as frank and complete; he brings out Mrs Fainall's latent generosity by reminding her of the truth of their past relationship, dissolving the bitterness she seemed to declare (with whatever disingenuous motives) to Mrs Marwood at the beginning of the Act. It is true that Mirabell knows he can win over Mrs Fainall because she still feels affection for him; on the other hand she does not resist his firm, implicit assumption that their relationship could never have ended in marriage. Mirabell admits his own culpability in a disagreeable affair; on the other hand he reminds Mrs Fainall of her equal responsibility in the phrase '*our* loves'. Mirabell shows Mrs Fainall the hollowness of the worldly wisdom she had exchanged with Mrs Marwood;[30] he has ceased to love her, but does not loathe her. Of course, at the same time, Mirabell's judgement of her is shrewd, and is confirmed by her acceptance of a future in which, secured (by his foresight) from the menace of Fainall, she can adopt the programme suggested by Mrs Marwood, and not refuse the sweets of life because they once must leave her, although in her heart she knows that one day she will be old, and fit only for the part of Lady Wishfort, withering in an affected bloom. Mrs Fainall is in these terms an affected wit, a false wit; but her assent to Mirabell's wishes indicates her recognition of his truth, and is the key to the ultimate success of Mirabell's endeavour to win the favour of Lady Wishfort herself. Congreve stresses that Mirabell has had experience, his maturity has been bought with a knowledge of suffering and a degree of guilt; but like Valentine in *Love for Love* he is generous, and is rewarded by the generosity of Mrs Fainall; in this sense it is possible to see Mirabell's career in the play as a demonstration of his reformation, closely contrasted to the degeneration of his opponent Fainall, and echoed by the natures of their respective mistresses, Mrs Marwood and Mrs Fainall.[31] This indicates little more than a crude outline, of course, since the centre of the design is Millamant. Mirabell's past experience of the disagreeable aspects of the World matters most because it has educated him to a mature awareness of the need for prudence, judiciousness, tolerance, and a shrewd insight into the base motives which men are heir to; without all this, generosity would aid Mirabell no more than it does Sir Wilfull, who has quantities of the spirit, in a raw condition, but who appears to Millamant, and even to Lady Wishfort, repellent.

Millamant's arrival completes Congreve's design of the Act; the

[30] II, 1–24.
[31] This is the central argument of Paul and Miriam Mueschke, *A New View of Congreve's Way of the World* (Michigan, 1958).

encounter between the bitter couple, Fainall and Mrs Marwood, is succeeded by that between the forgiving ex-lovers Mirabell and Mrs Fainall, and that in turn precedes the meeting of the witty, loving couple Mirabell and Millamant who will marry, and who embody the play's ideals. Millamant has more gaiety than Mirabell ('Sententious Mirabell! Prithee don't look with that violent and inflexible wise face') and indeed her entrance releases the comic spirit which has been hitherto suppressed in Act II. Congreve's genius in characterisation extends to the gayer characters; Millamant is impish, she deliberately exaggerates her affectations to provoke Mirabell, using the presence of Witwoud and Mincing to elude his efforts and to fill the stage with airy vitality; Mirabell reacts by exaggerating his own truly valuable capacity for seriousness, and like Rosalind Millamant instantly seizes on his slight falsity of tone, his dull apprehension of the mood:

> . . . Beauty the lover's gift! Lord, what is a lover, that it can give? Why, one makes lovers as fast as one pleases, and they live as long as one pleases, and they die as soon as one pleases; and then, if one pleases, one makes more. (II, 360–63)

Millamant is really in love, like Rosalind in *As You Like It*; and though she does not declare that her affection 'hath an unknown bottom, like the Bay of Portugal'[32] the whole effect of her performance depends upon the audience's recognition of the fact, so that it shares the joke against Mirabell and the secret joy of Millamant's possession of the experience. The audience will side with Millamant also over the matter of her tolerance of the herd of fools, recognising the element of jealousy in Mirabell's objection but also confident that Millamant is his equal in judgement, as she tantalises him with her wit. When she leaves him, the comic atmosphere has become so free and auspicious that he bursts out with a passionate exclamation:

> Think of you! To think of a whirlwind, though 'twere in a whirlwind, were a case of more steady contemplation: (II, 437–9)

The speech, as the images make plain, has a truly powerful intensity of feeling, the feeling which has been present throughout the scene with Millamant, which underlies all their witty exchanges. The point is crucial. They are not anaemic, a fop and a coquette, though they have breeding, wit, and tact; they are man and woman, and the major scenes of the play – involving Fainall and Mrs Marwood as well as Mirabell and Millamant – are passionate and powerful.

This fact is emphasised by the sharp contrast with the absurdity

[32] *As You Like It*, IV, i, 187–8.

of the postures Lady Wishfort adopts, with desperate yet unflagging energy; she has a Jonsonian ability to inflate herself into a simulacrum of a romantic heroine, but she remains a sort of female Epicure Mammon in her hopes, and a Volpone in her looks:

> Let me see the glass. Cracks, sayest thou? Why, I am arrantly flayed! I look like an old peeled wall! Thou must repair me Foible, before Sir Rowland comes ...   (III, 130–3)

Congreve's rich inheritance from Shakespearean and Jonsonian comedy is generously spent in *The Way of the World;* for if the grand strokes of caricature proclaim the influence of Jonson, the marvellously particular and complete identities of the comic characters owe much to Shakespeare's example. Lady Wishfort and Sir Wilfull can be moving as well as ridiculous, though the effect is momentary, like Sir Andrew Aguecheek in *Twelfth Night* melancholically confessing 'I was adored once too', or like Dogberry in *Much Ado* remembering that he has 'had losses'. Perhaps it is just these sad moments in the lives of the old (and mostly ridiculous) minor characters which bring them so completely to life, modifying the comic atmosphere from hilarity to a blend of melancholy so familiar elsewhere in the plays of Chekhov. In creating Lady Wishfort Congreve has drawn on the Nurse in *Romeo and Juliet*[33] as well as taking a full measure of the immediate original (created by Mrs Leigh), Lady Woodvil in *The Man of Mode*; but the poetic richness of Lady Wishfort's half-ridiculous, half-pitiable imposture of youth and outraged dignity owes something to Falstaff too:

> A cup! Save thee, and what a cup hast thou brought! Dost thou take me for a fairy, to drink out of an acorn?   (III, 25–6)

Sir Wilfull's part in the finale recalls that of Kastril in Act IV of *The Alchemist*, but Sir Wilfull brings from Shropshire a loam-footed honesty and a speech as richly flavoured as a nut or an apple, which eventually win him some credit (he is given greater reward by Henry Fielding, who draws on him for Squire Western in *Tom Jones*). In the magnificent first encounter between Sir Wilfull and his half-brother Witwoud, haunting echoes of Falstaff and Justice Shallow enrich the atmosphere as Sir Wilfull discloses that Witwoud 'lived with honest Pumplenose the attorney of Furnival's Inn';[34]

---

[33] Compare *Romeo and Juliet*, II, v, 147–51: 'Scurvy knave! I am none of his flirt-gills; I am none of his skains-mates. And thou must stand by too, and suffer every knave to use me at his pleasure?' with Lady Wishfort's 'Audacious villain! Handle me! Would he durst! Frippery! Old frippery! Was there ever such a foul-mouthed fellow?'

[34] See *2 Henry IV*, III, ii, 13–14: 'I was once of Clement's Inn; where I think they will talk of mad Shallow yet.'

Falstaffian images occur to Witwoud in observing that Sir Wilfull's foreign tour will make him 'refined, like a Dutch skipper from a whale-fishing'. It is perhaps inevitable, as well as appropriate and traditional, that the hilarious scene of intoxication in Act IV (always the farcical climax in Jonsonian comedy) should be dominated by this embodiment of instinct and appetite, vital, anarchic, close to the well-springs of the comic spirit, including fragments of Sir Toby Belch's memorable performance[35] of drunken caterwauling, making 'an alehouse of my lady's house'.

Sir Wilfull's earthy saturnalian revels meet with a reaction from Millamant which we may associate with her reaction to Mirabell's provisos for their marriage:

MIRABELL
    . . . *Item*, when you shall be breeding—
MILLAMANT
    Ah! Name it not.
MIRABELL
    Which may be presumed, with a blessing on our endeavours—
MILLAMANT
    Odious endeavours!   (IV, 223–8)

Millamant, notwithstanding such affected attitudes, cannot withstand instinct and inclination; she seeks only to temper instinct with order, not to suppress it – and judging by Sir Wilfull's expression of instinct, there is no suppressing it anyway:

MILLAMANT
    Your pardon madam, I can stay no longer – Sir Wilfull grows very powerful – egh! How he smells! I shall be overcome if I stay. Come, cousin.
LADY WISHFORT
    Smells! He would poison a tallow chandler and his family. Beastly creature, I know not what to do with him. (IV, 376–80)

Lady Wishfort, of course, has never known how to reconcile the demands of human nature with the rules of society, vacillating always between attenuated politeness:

    I hope you do not think me prone to any iteration of nuptials.
                                                      (IV, 464–5)

and grossly extravagant abuse:

    Go! Go! That I took from washing of old gauze and weaving of dead hair, with a bleak blue nose, over a chafing dish of starved embers, and dining behind a traverse rag, in a shop no bigger than a bird-cage. Go, go, starve again! Do! Do!   (V, 3–7)

[35] *Twelfth Night*, II, iii.

Lady Wishfort never has balance, Millamant never loses it, not even at the moment of triumph:

> Why does not the man take me? Would you have me give myself
> to you over again? (V, 536–7)

Millamant's poise is ideal, she achieves personal fulfilment without infringing the laws of society; but the play as a whole shows that her fulfilment is dependent on the skill of Mirabell, and is achieved through confronting experience of a more serious and widely inclusive range than the conventions of comedy normally allow. If Congreve succeeds, in *The Way of the World*, in modifying the art of comedy to make its morality more inclusive and reconciliatory, less ideal and remote, he remains faithful to the spirit of romantic comedy in its central affirmation of the power of love: for the play shows how Mirabell imposes on the cynically realistic way of the world the more generous vision of the art of comedy. *The Way of the World* is not an ironic title, it is reconciliatory; properly understood, the play is a celebration.

THE SOURCES

An editor required to produce a complete account of the sources of *The Way of The World* might be forgiven for answering, with Benedick, that he would rather go on the slightest errand to the Antipodes, fetch a toothpicker from the farthest inch of Asia, or a hair off the Great Cham's beard. In this play Congreve has drawn on a great range of comedy, from Plautus and Terence to Etherege, Molière, Shadwell, and Southerne. The theme is indicated by the epigraph from Horace's second satire in his *Satires, I*, the fate of adulterers and the fears of a guilty woman for the loss of her reputation. This didactic intent draws attention to the debt to Jonsonian critical comedy – especially *The Devil Is An Ass* (1616), *Bartholomew Fair* (1614), and *The Silent Woman* (1609). In the first-named of these, Fitzdottrel is disposed to treat his wife unfairly and desert her; Wittipol causes Fitzdottrel to convey her estate to Wittipol's friend Manly, and hence reduces Fitzdottrel to a state of financial dependence on his wife, and effects a *modus vivendi* for all parties.[36] In the second play, the wedding licence in the black box is the means to an 'artful solution of the fable', like the casket in Plautus' *Cistellaria;* and in the third, *The Silent Woman*, Truewit warns Morose before his marriage that 'This, too, with whom you are to marry, may have made a conveyance of her virginity beforehand, as your wise widdowes doe of their states, before they marry' (II, ii, 140). Real-life instances of this situation in the Jacobean period have been recorded, to extend Congreve's possible sources to infinity.[37]

The debt to Jonson is a testimony to Congreve's classical and conservative inclination, since Jonson himself 'Englished' Roman and Greek comedy. In complex romantic intrigue and subtlety of character and dialogue Congreve is indebted, as he himself claims, to Terence, though Terence's plays are innocent of the didactic impulse which Horatian non-dramatic satire passed on to Jonson and hence to Congreve. There can be little doubt that the Horatian epigraph is intended as an indication of the critical element in the comedy, while the central figures Mirabell and Millamant originate in Benedick and Beatrice in *Much Ado About Nothing* as well as in

[36] See Kathleen Lynch, *The Social Mode of Restoration Comedy* (London, 1926), pp. 192–3.
[37] See L. G. Salingar, 'Farce and Fashion in *The Silent Woman*', *Essays and Studies* (London, 1967).

the many gay couples of earlier Restoration comedies.[38] The proviso scene had been invented by Honoré D'Urfé (*L'Astrée*, 1607–27) and Congreve borrows verbally from Dryden's *Secret Love* for the scene. There are other echoes of Dryden's *Marriage à la Mode* and *The Wild Gallant*, and there is a general debt in structure and style to Etherege's *The Man of Mode*, and Congreve even inherited two of the original actors of that play to perform similar roles in his own comedy. There are memories of Sir Toby Belch and Falstaff and other buffoons in Sir Wilfull, and also of Peregrine in Brome's comedy *The Antipodes*; Lady Wishfort is compounded of memories of Etherege's Lady Woodvil but also of Jonson (Morose, Volpone, Ursula, Face) and Shakespeare (the Nurse in *Romeo and Juliet*, Falstaff). Petulant derives from Jonsonian quarrellers and from Nym in *Henry IV*. There are perhaps debts to Shadwell; *Bury Fair* (1689) may have suggested Lady Wishfort's ridiculous education of her daughter,[39] though Molière's *L'École des Femmes* is a more obvious source, and *The Amorous Bigot* (1690) may have suggested the Sir Rowland episode – though this is a variation on the gulling of Malvolio, itself an ancient *lazzo*.

Like Congreve's earlier comedies, *The Way of the World* has a strictly formalised design and all its characters are types from the comedy of manners; what is more, Congreve's own plays provide the most important source for this last masterpiece, which evolves from them. It is a sign of his greater maturity here that the magisterial Shakespearean comic language is absorbed into the texture of his play without control being lost; and the use of Shakespearean and Jonsonian material here suggests the unattainable ideal to which Congreve aspired, and the essentially English character of his art.

[38] The fuller history of their ancestry is in J. H. Smith, *The Gay Couple in Restoration Comedy* (Cambridge, Mass., 1948).
[39] Kathleen Lynch, ed., *The Way of the World* (London, 1965), p. xiv.

THE TEXT

The copy-text for this edition is the first quarto of 1700 in the British Museum. This has been collated with the second quarto of 1706 and the editions of 1710 and 1719. I have consulted the editions of Montague Summers (London, 1923), Kathleen Lynch (London, 1965), and Herbert Davis (London, 1967). Spelling and punctuation have been modernised. Textual notes are printed at the foot of the relevant page; *Q1* refers to the edition of 1700, *Q2* to that of 1706, *W1* to the collected edition of 1710, and *W2* to that of 1719; *Ww* indicates agreement between readings in the two editions of 1710 and 1719.

FURTHER READING

The following books and articles are suggested in addition to those already mentioned in the introduction:

On Congreve

E. L. Avery, *Congreve's Plays on the Eighteenth Century Stage* (New York, 1952).

N. N. Holland, *The First Modern Comedies* (Cambridge, Mass., 1959).

W. H. Van Voris, *The Cultivated Stance* (London 1966).

Brian Morris ed., *William Congreve: Mermaid Critical Commentary* (London 1971).

Harold Love, *Congreve,* (Oxford 1974).

Peter Holland, *The Ornament of Action* (Cambridge, 1978).

Aubrey Williams, *An Approach to Congreve* (New Haven 1979).

T. W. Craik, 'Congreve as a Shakespearean', *Poetry and Drama 1570-1700,* ed. A. Coleman and A. Hammond (London, 1981).

Alexander Lindsay and Howard Erskine-Hill eds, *Congreve: The Critical Heritage* (London, 1989).

Julie Peters, *Congreve, the Drama, and the Printed Word* (Stanford, 1990).

On Restoration Comedy and Drama in general

Allardyce, Nicoll, *A History of English Drama 1660-1900.* Vol. 1 (London, 1961).

Eric Bentley, *The Life of the Drama* (London, 1965), especially the chapter on comedy.

J. R. Brown and Bernard Harris eds., *Restoration Theatre,* Stratford-upon-Avon Studies 6 (London, 1965).

John Loftis ed., *Restoration Drama,* Galaxy Books (New York, 1966).

E. Miner ed., *Restoration Dramatists,* Twentieth Century Views (Englewood Cliffs. 1966).

Richard Leacroft, *The Development of the English Playhouse* (London 1973).

John Loftis et al., *The Revels History of Drama in English,* Vol. 5 (London. 1976).

Arthur H. Scouten and Robert D. Hume, '"Restoration Comedy" and its audiences 1660-1776'. *Yearbook of English Studies* volume 10, (1980), pp.45-69.

Jocelyn Powell, *Restoration Theatre Production* (London, 1984).

Judith Milhaus and Robert D. Hume. *Producible Interpretation* (Carbondale, Illinois, 1985).

Harold Weber, *The Restoration Rake Hero* (Madison, Wisconsin, 1985).

Retta M. Taney, *Restoration Revivals on the British Stage 1944-79* (London 1985).

J. L. Styan, *Restoration Comedy in Performance* (Cambridge 1986).

Edward Burns, *Restoration Comedy, Crises of Desire and Identity* (London 1987).

Julie Peters, 'Things Governed by Words', *English Studies,* pp.142-53 (1987).

THE
Way of the World,
A
COMEDY.

As it is ACTED

AT THE

Theatre in *Lincoln's-Inn-Fields*,

BY

His Majesty's Servants.

Written by Mr. *CONGREVE*.

Audire est Operæ pretium, procedere recte
Qui mœchis non vultis ———
——— *Metuat doti deprensa.* ———

Hor. Sat. 2. l. 1.
Ibid.

LONDON:

Printed for *Jacob Tonson*, within *Gray's-Inn-Gate* next
Gray's-Inn-Lane. 1700.

To the Right Honourable
RALPH
Earl of MONTAGUE, &c.

MY LORD,

Whether the world will arraign me of vanity, or not, that I
have presumed to dedicate this comedy to your Lordship, I am
yet in doubt: though it may be it is some degree of vanity even
to doubt of it. One who has at any time had the honour of your   5
Lordship's conversation, cannot be supposed to think very
meanly of that which he would prefer to your perusal; yet it
were to incur the imputation of too much sufficiency, to
pretend to such a merit as might abide the test of your Lordship's censure.   10

Whatever value may be wanting to this play while yet it is
mine, will be sufficiently made up to it, when it is once
become your Lordship's; and it is my security, that I cannot
have overrated it more by my dedication than your Lordship
will dignify it by your patronage.   15

That it succeeded on the stage, was almost beyond my expectation; for but little of it was prepared for that general taste
which seems now to be predominant in the palates of our
audience.

Those characters which are meant to be ridiculous in most of   20
our comedies are of fools so gross, that in my humble opinion
they should rather disturb than divert the well-natured and re-
flecting part of an audience; they are rather objects of charity

---

20 *ridiculous* Q1 (ridiculed Q2, Ww)

Dedication Ralph Earl of Montague. Ralph Montague (1638–1709) was
created Earl in 1689, having actively supported the deposition of James
II and the installing of William III, after a long and intricate political
career; he became Duke of Montague in 1705. He made two fortunes
by marriage, his second marriage in 1692 to the Duchess of Newcastle
being notable for the fact that she was very insane indeed, and had
vowed only to marry a crowned head. Montague consequently presented himself to her as the Emperor of China, and was accepted!
Whether this remarkable circumstance was in Congreve's mind when
devising the Sir Rowland episode in the present play must remain a
matter for conjecture.

7 *prefer* offer   8 *sufficiency* ability

3

than contempt; and instead of moving our mirth, they ought
very often to excite our compassion. 25

This reflection moved me to design some characters which
should appear ridiculous, not so much through a natural folly
(which is incorrigible, and therefore not proper for the stage) as
through an affected wit: a wit, which at the same time that it is
affected, is also false. As there is some difficulty in the formation 30
of a character of this nature, so there is some hazard which
attends the progress of its success upon the stage; for many
come to a play so over-charged with criticism that they very
often let fly their censure, when through their rashness they
have mistaken their aim. This I had occasion lately to observe; 35
for this play has been acted two or three days before some of
these hasty judges could find the leisure to distinguish betwixt
the character of a Witwoud and a Truewit.

I must beg your Lordship's pardon for this digression from
the true course of this epistle; but that it may not seem al- 40
together impertinent, I beg that I may plead the occasion of it,
in part of that excuse of which I stand in need, for recommending
this comedy to your protection. It is only by the countenance
of your Lordship, and the *few* so qualified, that such who write
with care and pains can hope to be distinguished; for the pro- 45
stituted name of *poet* promiscuously levels all that bear it.

Terence, the most correct writer in the world, had a Scipio
and a Laelius, if not to assist him, at least to support him in his

---

38 *a Witwoud and a Truewit.* Witwoud in *The Way of the World* exempli-
fies the absurdity of affectation, and the ridiculous pretension to
intelligence and judgement, common to the fools in the play. Truewit
in Ben Jonson's *The Silent Woman* perceives and exposes—though
rather cruelly—the false values and perverse conduct of the misanthrope
Morose. Though Truewit has intelligence, ingenuity, and understanding based on a scholarly education, and Dryden thought him the best of
Jonson's characters of gentlemen, he also thought Truewit inferior in
gallantry and civility to gentlemen of his own time, which Dryden held
to be 'much more courtly' ('Defence of the Epilogue' in John Dryden,
Of Dramatic Poesy and other Critical Essays, ed. G. Watson [London,
1962], I, 180). Pope, with unusual misjudgement, was to repeat the
objection that Congreve's fools had too much wit:

> Observe how seldom ev'n the best succeed:
> Tell me if Congreve's Fools are Fools indeed?
>
> (*Imitations of Horace*, Ep. II, i, 287–8).

47–8 *a Scipio and a Laelius.* Terence's patrons, who gave him valuable
protection during his controversial career. Scipio Africanus was the
leader of an intellectual circle including Gaius Laelius, and Terence
soon gained admittance to it after arriving in Rome from Carthage.

reputation; and notwithstanding his extraordinary merit, it may
be their countenance was not more than necessary.   50

The purity of his style, the delicacy of his turns, and the
justness of his characters, were all of them beauties which the
greater part of his audience were incapable of tasting; some of
the coarsest strokes of Plautus, so severely censured by Horace,
were more likely to affect the multitude—such who come with   55
expectation to laugh out the last act of a play, and are better
entertained with two or three unseasonable jests than with the
artful solution of the *fable*.

As Terence excelled in his performances, so had he great
advantages to encourage his undertakings, for he built most on   60
the foundations of Menander; his plots were generally
modelled, and his characters ready drawn to his hand. He copied
Menander; and Menander had no less light in the formation
of his characters from the observations of Theophrastus, of
whom he was a disciple; and Theophrastus, it is known, was not   65
only the disciple, but the immediate successor of Aristotle, the
first and greatest judge of poetry. These were great models
to design by; and the further advantage which Terence posses-
sed towards giving his plays the due ornaments of purity of
style, and justness of manners, was not less considerable: from   70
the freedom of conversation, which was permitted him with
Laelius and Scipio, two of the greatest and most polite men of
his age. And indeed, the privilege of such a conversation is the
only certain means of attaining to the perfection of dialogue.

If it has happened in any part of this comedy that I have   75
gained a turn of style or expression more correct, or at least
more corrigible than in those which I have formerly written, I
must with equal pride and gratitude ascribe it to the honour of
your Lordship's admitting me into your conversation, and that
of a society where everybody else was so well worthy of you, in   80
your retirement last summer from the town; for it was immediately after that this comedy was written. If I have failed in
my performance it is only to be regretted, where there were so
many not inferior either to a Scipio or a Laelius, that there

---

56 *laugh out* Q1, some copies of Q2 (laugh at Q2, Ww)

58 *fable* plot
61 *Menander*. Dramatist, writer of Greek New Comedy, drawn on by
   Terence in composing his own plays.
65 *Theophrastus*. Greek author of non-dramatic 'characters' and the model
   for English seventeenth-century writers of 'characters', such as Earle
   and Overbury.

should be one wanting, equal to the capacity of a Terence.   85

If I am not mistaken, poetry is almost the only art which has not yet laid claim to your Lordship's patronage. Architecture, and painting, to the great honour of our country, have flourished under your influence and protection. In the mean time poetry, the eldest sister of all arts and parent of most, seems to   90 have resigned her birthright by having neglected to pay her duty to your Lordship, and by permitting others of a later extraction to prepossess that place in your esteem to which none can pretend a better title. Poetry, in its nature, is sacred to the good and great; the relation between them is reciprocal, and   95 they are ever propitious to it. It is the privilege of poetry to address to them, and it is their prerogative alone to give it protection.

This received maxim is a general apology for all writers who consecrate their labours to great men; but I could wish at this   100 time that this address were exempted from the common pretense of all dedications; and that as I can distinguish your Lordship even among the most deserving, so this offering might become remarkable by some particular instance of respect which should assure your Lordship that I am, with all due sense   105 of your extreme worthiness and humanity.

MY LORD,
Your Lordship's
Most Obedient
and Most Humble   110
Servant,
WILL. CONGREVE

---

85 *to the capacity of* Q1, Q2 (in capacity to Ww)

87 *Architecture.* Montague built two great houses, Boughton House in Northamptonshire after the model of Versailles and Montagu House, Bloomsbury, also in the French style.

PROLOGUE
Spoken by Mr. Betterton

Of those few fools, who with ill stars are cursed,
Sure scribbling fools, called poets, fare the worst;
For they're a sort of fools which Fortune makes
And after she has made 'em fools, forsakes.
With Nature's oafs 'tis quite a different case,   5
For Fortune favours all her idiot race;
In her own nest the cuckoo eggs we find,
O'er which she broods to hatch the changeling kind.
No portion for her own she has to spare,
So much she dotes on her adopted care.   10
   Poets are bubbles, by the town drawn in,
Suffered at first some trifling stakes to win:
But what unequal hazards do they run!
Each time they write they venture all they've won;
The squire that's buttered still is sure to be undone. 15
This author heretofore has found your favour,
But pleads no merit from his past behaviour.
To build on that might prove a vain presumption
Should grants, to poets made, admit resumption;
And in Parnassus he must lose his seat   20
If that be found a forfeited estate.
   He owns, with toil he wrought the following scenes,
But if they're naught ne'er spare him for his pains,
Damn him the more; have no commiseration
For dullness on mature deliberation.   25
He swears he'll not resent one hissed-off scene
Nor, like those peevish wits, his play maintain,
Who, to assert their sense, your taste arraign.
Some plot we think he has, and some new thought;
Some humour too, no farce—but that's a fault.   30
Satire, he thinks, you ought not to expect:
For so reformed a town, who dares correct?
To please this time has been his sole pretence;

11 *bubbles* victims of fraud
15 *buttered* lavishly flattered
32 *so reformed a town* alluding to the Puritan attack, Collier's *A Short
   View of the Profaneness and Immorality of the English Stage* (1698)

He'll not instruct less it should give offence.
Should he by chance a knave or fool expose,   35
That hurts none here: sure here are none of those.
In short our play shall (with your leave to show it)
Give you one instance of a passive poet
Who to your judgements yields all resignation;
So save or damn, after your own discretion.   40

DRAMATIS PERSONAE

Men

FAINALL, *in love with Mrs. Marwood*	*Mr. Betterton*
MIRABELL, *in love with Mrs. Millamant*	*Mr. Verbruggen*
WITWOUD, PETULANT, } *followers of Mrs. Millamant*	{ *Mr. Bowen* *Mr. Bowman*
SIR WILFULL WITWOUD, *half-brother to Witwoud, and nephew to Lady Wishfort*	} *Mr. Underhill*
WAITWELL, *servant to Mirabell*	*Mr. Bright*

Women

LADY WISHFORT, *enemy to Mirabell for having falsely pretended love to her*	} *Mrs. Leigh*
MRS MILLAMANT, *a fine lady, niece to Lady Wishfort, and loves Mirabell*	} *Mrs. Bracegirdle*
MRS. MARWOOD, *friend to Mr. Fainall, and likes Mirabell*	} *Mrs. Barry*
MRS. FAINALL, *daughter to Lady Wishfort and wife to Fainall, formerly friend to Mirabell*	} *Mrs. Bowman*
FOIBLE, *woman to Lady Wishfort*	*Mrs. Willis*
MINCING, *woman to Mrs. Millamant*	*Mrs. Prince*

DANCERS, FOOTMEN, AND ATTENDANTS

SCENE LONDON

The time equal to that of the presentation

FAINALL The names identify character types; Fainall 'feigns all'.
MIRABELL 'admirable', and also perhaps 'an admirer of female beauty'
WITWOUD Compare Jonson's character *Sir Politic Would-be* for this kind of name.
MILLAMANT i.e. she has a thousand lovers; see II, 360–3

THE WAY OF THE WORLD
A Comedy

Act I, Scene i

A Chocolate-house

MIRABELL *and* FAINALL, [*rising from cards*]. BETTY *waiting*

MIRABELL

You are a fortunate man, Mr. Fainall.

FAINALL

Have we done?

MIRABELL

What you please. I'll play on to entertain you.

FAINALL

No, I'll give you your revenge another time, when you are
not so indifferent; you are thinking of something else now,   5
and play too negligently; the coldness of a losing gamester
lessens the pleasure of the winner. I'd no more play with a
man that slighted his ill fortune than I'd make love to a woman
who undervalued the loss of her reputation.

MIRABELL

You have a taste extremely delicate, and are for refining on   10
your pleasures.

FAINALL

Prithee, why so reserved? Something has put you out of
humour.

MIRABELL

Not at all; I happen to be grave today, and you are gay:
that's all.   15

FAINALL

Confess, Millamant and you quarrelled last night after I left
you. My fair cousin has some humours that would tempt the
patience of a Stoic. What, some coxcomb came in, and was
well received by her, while you were by.

MIRABELL

Witwoud and Petulant; and what was worse, her aunt, your   20
wife's mother, my evil genius; or to sum up all in her own
name, my old Lady Wishfort came in.

17 *humours* moods

11

FAINALL

Oh there it is then! She has a lasting passion for you, and with reason. What, then my wife was there?

MIRABELL

Yes, and Mrs. Marwood and three or four more, whom I   25
never saw before. Seeing me, they all put on their grave faces, whispered one another, then complained aloud of the vapours, and after fell into a profound silence.

FAINALL

They had a mind to be rid of you.

MIRABELL

For which reason I resolved not to stir. At last the good old   30
lady broke through her painful taciturnity, with an invective against long visits. I would not have understood her, but Millamant joining in the argument, I rose and with a constrained smile told her, I thought nothing was so easy as to know when a visit began to be troublesome. She reddened   35
and I withdrew, without expecting her reply.

FAINALL

You were to blame to resent what she spoke only in compliance with her aunt.

MIRABELL

She is more mistress of herself than to be under the necessity of such a resignation.   40

FAINALL

What? Though half her fortune depends upon her marrying with my lady's approbation?

MIRABELL

I was then in such a humour that I should have been better pleased if she had been less discreet.

FAINALL

Now I remember, I wonder not they were weary of you; last   45
night was one of their cabal-nights. They have 'em three

28 *vapours* supposed exhalations from the organs of the body causing depression or nervous disorders

41 *fortune*. Millamant's fortune of £12,000 is rather larger than might have been likely for a lady in her social position in 1700, according to John Loftis, *Comedy and Society from Congreve to Fielding* (Stanford, 1959), pp. 46–8. This shows that traditional romantic spirit informs Congreve's design.

46 *cabal-nights*. The term is humorously exaggerated; serious political intrigue does not occupy the ladies. There is a reminiscence of *The Silent Woman*, I, i, where Truewit and Dauphine mockingly discuss the 'collegiate ladies'.

times a week, and meet by turns at one another's apartments, where they come together like the coroner's inquest, to sit upon the murdered reputations of the week. You and I are excluded, and it was once proposed that all the male sex 50 should be excepted; but somebody moved that, to avoid scandal, there might be one man of the community; upon which motion Witwoud and Petulant were enrolled members.

MIRABELL

And who may have been the foundress of this sect? My Lady Wishfort, I warrant, who publishes her detestation of man- 55 kind; and full of the vigour of fifty-five, declares for a friend and ratafia, and let posterity shift for itself, she'll breed no more.

FAINALL

The discovery of your sham addresses to her, to conceal your love to her niece, has provoked this separation. Had you 60 dissembled better, things might have continued in the state of nature.

MIRABELL

I did as much as man could, with any reasonable conscience. I proceeded to the very last act of flattery with her, and was guilty of a song in her commendation; nay, I got a friend to 65 put her into a lampoon, and compliment her with the imputation of an affair with a young fellow, which I carried so far that I told her the malicious town took notice that she was grown fat of a sudden; and when she lay in of a dropsy, persuaded her she was reported to be in labour. The devil's in't, 70 if an old woman is to be flattered further, unless a man should endeavour downright personally to debauch her: and that my virtue forbade me. But for the discovery of this amour, I am indebted to your friend, or your wife's friend, Mrs. Marwood. 75

FAINALL

What should provoke her to be your enemy, without she has made you advances which you have slighted? Women do not easily forgive omissions of that nature.

MIRABELL

She was always civil to me, till of late. I confess I am not one of those coxcombs who are apt to interpret a woman's good 80

73–4 *this amour* ed. (that amour Q1)
76 *without she* Q1, Q2 (unless she Ww)

57 *ratafia* cherry brandy made with peach stones and apricot stones
57 *shift* take care

manners to her prejudice, and think that she who does not refuse 'em everything, can refuse 'em nothing.

FAINALL

You are a gallant man, Mirabell; and though you may have cruelty enough not to satisfy a lady's longing, you have too much generosity not to be tender of her honour. Yet you speak with an indifference which seems to be affected, and confesses you are conscious of a negligence.   85

MIRABELL

You pursue the argument with a distrust that seems to be unaffected, and confesses you are conscious of a concern, for which the lady is more indebted to you than your wife.   90

FAINALL

Fie, fie, friend! If you grow censorious I must leave you. I'll look upon the gamesters in the next room.

MIRABELL

Who are they?

FAINALL

Petulant and Witwoud. [*to* BETTY] Bring me some chocolate.

Exit

MIRABELL

Betty, what says your clock?   95

BETTY

Turned of the last canonical hour sir.   *Exit*

MIRABELL

How pertinently the jade answers me! Ha? Almost one o'clock! (*looking on his watch*) Oh, y'are come!

Enter a SERVANT

Well, is the grand affair over? You have been something tedious.   100

SERVANT

Sir, there's such coupling at Pancras that they stand behind one another as 'twere in a country dance. Ours was the last couple to lead up; and no hopes appearing of dispatch, besides, the parson growing hoarse, we were afraid his lungs would have failed before it came to our turn; so we drove   105

---

90 *than your wife* Q1, Q2 (than is your wife Ww)

---

96 *canonical hour.* 8 a.m. to noon were the hours during which legal marriages in church could take place.

101 *Pancras.* Summers cites *The Modish Wife* (1676) V, iii: 'What think you of taking a Coach to *Pancras*-Church . . . for that is a place of Priviledge and Liberty to Marry without Licences, and at any time'.

round to Duke's Place and there they were riveted in a trice.

MIRABELL

So, so, you are sure they are married.

SERVANT

Married and bedded sir: I am witness.

MIRABELL

Have you the certificate?   110

SERVANT

Here it is sir.

MIRABELL

Has the tailor brought Waitwell's clothes home, and the new liveries?

SERVANT

Yes sir.

MIRABELL

That's well. Do you go home again, d'ye hear, and adjourn   115
the consummation till farther order. Bid Waitwell shake his ears, and Dame Partlet rustle up her feathers, and meet me at one o'clock by Rosamond's Pond, that I may see her before she returns to her lady; and as you tender your ears, be secret.   *Exit* SERVANT   120

Enter FAINALL [*and* BETTY]

FAINALL

Joy of your success, Mirabell; you look pleased.

MIRABELL

Ay, I have been engaged in a matter of some sort of mirth which is not yet ripe for discovery. I am glad this is not a cabal-night. I wonder, Fainall, that you who are married, and of consequence should be discreet, will suffer your wife to   125
be of such a party.

FAINALL

Faith, I am not jealous. Besides, most who are engaged are women and relations; and for the men, they are of a kind too contemptible to give scandal.

115 *d'ye* ed. (d'ee Q1) this emendation followed through the text

---

106 *Duke's Place* in Aldgate, now Duke Street. St James's Church there was notorious for irregular marriages, vulgarly called Fleet weddings (Summers).
117 *Dame Partlet* wife of Chanticleer in the fable; see Chaucer, *The Nun's Priest's Tale*.
118 *Rosamond's Pond* a favourite meeting-place in St James's Park around which Charles II planted groves (Lynch)

MIRABELL

I am of another opinion. The greater the coxcomb, always 130
the more the scandal; for a woman who is not a fool can have
but one reason for associating with a man that is.

FAINALL

Are you jealous as often as you see Witwoud entertained by
Millamant?

MIRABELL

Of her understanding I am, if not of her person. 135

FAINALL

You do her wrong; for to give her her due, she has wit.

MIRABELL

She has beauty enough to make any man think so, and complaisance enough not to contradict him who shall tell her so.

FAINALL

For a passionate lover, methinks you are a man somewhat too
discerning in the failings of your mistress. 140

MIRABELL

And for a discerning man, somewhat too passionate a
lover; for I like her with all her faults, nay, like her for her
faults. Her follies are so natural, or so artful, that they
become her; and those affectations which in another woman
would be odious, serve but to make her more agreeable. I'll 145
tell thee Fainall, she once used me with that insolence, that in
revenge I took her to pieces, sifted her, and separated her
failings; I studied 'em, and got 'em by rote. The catalogue
was so large, that I was not without hopes, one day or other to
hate her heartily; to which end I so used myself to think of 150
'em, that at length, contrary to my design and expectation,
they gave me every hour less and less disturbance, till in a
few days it became habitual to me to remember 'em without
being displeased. They are now grown as familiar to me as
my own frailties; and in all probability in a little time longer 155
I shall like 'em as well.

FAINALL

Marry her, marry her! Be half as well acquainted with her
charms as you are with her defects, and my life on't, you are
your own man again.

MIRABELL

Say you so? 160

132 *man that is* Q1, Q2 (man who is one Ww)

---

135 *understanding* intellect; capacity to comprehend and judge
159 *your own man* heart-free, not in love

FAINALL
  Ay, ay, I have experience: I have a wife, and so forth.

Enter MESSENGER

MESSENGER
  Is one Squire Witwoud here?
BETTY
  Yes; what's your business?
MESSENGER
  I have a letter for him from his brother Sir Wilfull, which
  I am charged to deliver into his own hands.   165
BETTY
  He's in the next room, friend – that way.   *Exit* MESSENGER
MIRABELL
  What, is the chief of that noble family in town, Sir Wilfull
  Witwoud?
FAINALL
  He is expected today. Do you know him?
MIRABELL
  I have seen him, he promises to be an extraordinary person. I   170
  think you have the honour to be related to him.
FAINALL
  Yes; he is half-brother to this Witwoud by a former wife,
  who was sister to my Lady Wishfort, my wife's mother. If
  you marry Millamant you must call cousins too.
MIRABELL
  I had rather be his relation than his acquaintance.   175
FAINALL
  He comes to town in order to equip himself for travel.
MIRABELL
  For travel! Why, the man that I mean is above forty!
FAINALL
  No matter for that; 'tis for the honour of England that all
  Europe should know we have blockheads of all ages.
MIRABELL
  I wonder there is not an act of parliament to save the credit   180
  of the nation and prohibit the exportation of fools.
FAINALL
  By no means, 'tis better as 'tis. 'Tis better to trade with a
  little loss, than to be quite eaten up with being overstocked.
MIRABELL
  Pray, are the follies of this knight-errant and those of the
  squire his brother anything related?   185

FAINALL

Not at all; Witwoud grows by the knight like a medlar grafted on a crab; one will melt in your mouth, and t'other set your teeth on edge; one is all pulp and the other all core.

MIRABELL

So one will be rotten before he be ripe, and the other will be   190
rotten without ever being ripe at all.

FAINALL

Sir Wilfull is an odd mixture of bashfulness and obstinacy; but when he's drunk he's as loving as the monster in *The Tempest*, and much after the same manner. To give t'other his due, he has something of good nature, and does not   195
always want wit.

MIRABELL

Not always; but as often as his memory fails him, and his commonplace of comparisons. He is a fool with a good memory and some few scraps of other folks' wit. He is one whose conversation can never be approved, yet it is now and   200
then to be endured. He has indeed one good quality, he is not exceptious; for he so passionately affects the reputation of understanding raillery, that he will construe an affront into a jest, and call downright rudeness and ill language satire and fire.   205

FAINALL

If you have a mind to finish his picture, you have an opportunity to do it at full length. Behold the original.

Enter WITWOUD

WITWOUD

Afford me your compassion, my dears; pity me Fainall, Mirabell, pity me!

MIRABELL

I do, from my soul.   210

194 *t'other* ed. (the t'other Q1, Q2)

---

186 *medlar* a sort of apple, eaten when decayed to a soft pulpy state; see *As You Like It*, III, ii, 108-10: 'for you'll be rotten ere you be half ripe, and that's the right virtue of the medlar.'
187 *crab* a sour wild apple, proverbial for its tartness
193-4 *monster in The Tempest* Purcell composed new music in 1690 for the highly popular Dryden-Davenant opera based on Shakespeare's play
198 *commonplace* a commonplace book, in which memorable sayings and verses were recorded.
202 *exceptious* disposed to make objections

FAINALL

Why, what's the matter?

WITWOUD

No letters for me, Betty?

BETTY

Did not the messenger bring you one but now, sir?

WITWOUD

Ay, but no other?

BETTY

No sir. 215

WITWOUD

That's hard, that's very hard. A messenger, a mule, a beast of
burden, he has brought me a letter from the fool my
brother, as heavy as a panegyric in a funeral sermon, or a
copy of commendatory verses from one poet to another.
And what's worse, 'tis as sure a forerunner of the author 220
as an epistle dedicatory.

MIRABELL

A fool, and your brother, Witwoud!

WITWOUD

Ay, ay, my half-brother. My half-brother he is, no nearer,
upon honour.

MIRABELL

Then 'tis possible he may be but half a fool. 225

WITWOUD

Good, good, Mirabell *le drôle*! Good, good, hang him, don't
let's talk of him. Fainall, how does your lady? Gad, I say
anything in the world to get this fellow out of my head. I beg
pardon that I should ask a man of pleasure, and the town, a
question at once so foreign and domestic. But I talk like an 230
old maid at a marriage, I don't know what I say; but she's
the best woman in the world.

FAINALL

'Tis well you don't know what you say, or else your commendation would go near to make me either vain or jealous.

WITWOUD

No man in town lives well with a wife but Fainall: your 235
judgement Mirabell?

MIRABELL

You had better step and ask his wife if you would be
credibly informed.

213 *the messenger* Q1, Q2 (a messenger Ww)
231 *but she's* Q1, Q2, W1 (she's W2)

WITWOUD

Mirabell.

MIRABELL

Ay.   240

WITWOUD

My dear, I ask ten thousand pardons – Gad I have forgot what I was going to say to you.

MIRABELL

I thank you heartily, heartily.

WITWOUD

No, but prithee excuse me, my memory is such a memory.

MIRABELL

Have a care of such apologies, Witwoud; for I never knew a   245
fool but he affected to complain either of the spleen or his memory.

FAINALL

What have you done with Petulant?

WITWOUD

He's reckoning his money – my money it was. I have no luck today.   250

FAINALL

You may allow him to win of you at play, for you are sure to be too hard for him at repartee. Since you monopolise the wit that is between you, the fortune must be his of course.

MIRABELL

I don't find that Petulant confesses the superiority of wit to be your talent, Witwoud.   255

WITWOUD

Come, come, you are malicious now, and would breed debates. Petulant's my friend, and a very honest fellow, and a very pretty fellow, and has a smattering – faith and troth a pretty deal – of an odd sort of a small wit. Nay, I'll do him justice. I'm his friend, I won't wrong him neither.   260
And if he had but any judgement in the world he would not be altogether contemptible. Come, come, don't detract from the merits of my friend.

FAINALL

You don't take your friend to be over-nicely bred.

WITWOUD

No no, hang him, the rogue has no manners at all, that I must   265

257–8 *honest fellow, and a very pretty* Q1, Q2, W1 (pretty fellow,
       and a very honest W2)
260 *him neither* Q1, Q2 (him Ww)
261 *had but any* Q1, Q2 (had any Ww)

own; no more breeding than a bum-baily, that I grant you.
'Tis pity, faith; the fellow has fire and life.

MIRABELL

What, courage?

WITWOUD

Hum, faith, I don't know as to that – I can't say as to that.
Yes, faith, in a controversy he'll contradict anybody.   270

MIRABELL

Though'twere a man whom he feared or a woman whom he
loved.

WITWOUD

Well, well, he does not always think before he speaks; we
have all our failings. You are too hard upon him, you are faith.
Let me excuse him. I can defend most of his faults, except   275
one or two. One he has, that's the truth on't, if he were my
brother I could not acquit him – that indeed I could wish
were otherwise.

MIRABELL

Ay, marry, what's that, Witwoud?

WITWOUD

Oh pardon me; expose the infirmities of my friend? No, my   280
dear, excuse me there.

FAINALL

What, I warrant he's insincere, or 'tis some such trifle.

WITWOUD

No, no, what if he be? 'Tis no matter for that; his wit will
excuse that. A wit should no more be sincere, than a woman
constant. One argues a decay of parts as t'other of beauty.   285

MIRABELL

Maybe you think him too positive?

WITWOUD

No, no, his being positive is an incentive to argument, and
keeps up conversation.

FAINALL

Too illiterate.

WITWOUD

That! That's his happiness. His want of learning gives him   290
the more opportunities to show his natural parts.

---

267 *pity, faith* Q1, Q2 (pity Ww)
282 *insincere* ed. (unsincere Q1, Q2, Ww)

---

266 *bum-baily* 'a bailiff of the meanest kind; one employed in arrests' (Dr
Johnson's Dictionary)

MIRABELL

He wants words.

WITWOUD

Ay; but I like him for that now; for his want of words gives
me the pleasure very often to explain his meaning.

FAINALL

He's impudent.   295

WITWOUD

No; that's not it.

MIRABELL

Vain.

WITWOUD

No.

MIRABELL

What, he speaks unseasonable truths sometimes, because
he has not wit enough to invent an evasion.   300

WITWOUD

Truths! Ha, ha, ha! No, no, since you will have it, I mean he
never speaks truth at all – that's all. He will lie like a
chambermaid, or a woman of quality's porter. Now that is a
fault.

Enter COACHMAN

COACHMAN

Is Master Petulant here, mistress?   305

BETTY

Yes.

COACHMAN

Three gentlewomen in the coach would speak with him.

FAINALL

Oh brave Petulant, three!

BETTY

I'll tell him.

COACHMAN

You must bring two dishes of chocolate and a glass of cinna-   310
mon-water.

Exit

WITWOUD

That should be for two fasting strumpets, and a bawd
troubled with wind. Now you may know what the three are.

307 *the coach* Q1, Q2 (a coach Ww)

310–11 *cinnamon-water* a digestive cordial flavoured with cinnamon

MIRABELL

You are very free with your friend's acquaintance.

WITWOUD

Ay, ay, friendship without freedom is as dull as love without   315
enjoyment, or wine without toasting; but to tell you a secret,
these are' trulls that he allows coach-hire, and something
more, by the week, to call on him once a day at public places.

MIRABELL

How!

WITWOUD

You shall see he won't go to 'em because there's no more   320
company here to take notice of him. Why this is nothing to
what he used to do; before he found out this way, I have
known him call for himself.

FAINALL

Call for himself? What dost thou mean?

WITWOUD

Mean? Why, he would slip you out of this chocolate-house,   325
just when you had been talking to him. As soon as your back
was turned, whip! He was gone. Then trip to his lodging,
clap on a hood and scarf, and mask, slap into a hackney-
coach, and drive hither to the door again in a trice; where he
would send in for himself, that I mean, call for himself, wait   330
for himself, nay and what's more, not finding himself,
sometimes leave a letter for himself.

MIRABELL

I confess this is something extraordinary. I believe he waits
for himself now, he is so long a-coming; Oh, I ask his
pardon.   335

Enter PETULANT

BETTY

Sir, the coach stays.

PETULANT

Well, well, I come. 'Sbud, a man had as good be a professed
midwife as a professed whoremaster at this rate. To be
knocked up, and raised, at all hours, and in all places! Pox on
'em! I won't come. D'ye hear, tell 'em I won't come. Let 'em   340
snivel and cry their hearts out.

FAINALL

You are very cruel, Petulant.

PETULANT

All's one, let it pass. I have a humour to be cruel.

317 *trulls that* Q1, Q2 (trulls whom Ww)

MIRABELL

I hope they are not persons of condition that you use at this
rate. 345

PETULANT

Condition? Condition's a dried fig, if I am not in humour.
By this hand, if they were your—a—a—your what-d'ye-call-
'ems themselves, they must wait or rub off, if I want appetite.

MIRABELL

What-d'ye-call-'ems! What are they, Witwoud?

WITWOUD

Empresses, my dear—by your what-d'ye-call-'ems he means 350
sultana queens.

PETULANT

Ay, Roxolanas.

MIRABELL

Cry you mercy.

FAINALL

Witwoud says they are—

PETULANT

What does he say th'are? 355

WITWOUD

I? Fine ladies I say.

PETULANT

Pass on, Witwoud. Harkee, by this light, his relations: two
co-heiresses his cousins, and an old aunt, that loves caterwauling better than a conventicle.

WITWOUD

Ha, ha, ha! I had a mind to see how the rogue would come 360
off—ha, ha, ha. Gad I can't be angry with him, if he said
they were my mother and my sisters.

MIRABELL

No!

WITWOUD

No; the rogue's wit and readiness of invention charm me;
dear Petulant. 365

358 *that loves* Q1, Q2 (who loves Ww)

---

344 *condition* gentle birth
352 *Roxolanas.* Roxolana is the wife of Sultan Solyman the Magnificent in
Davenant's *The Siege of Rhodes.*
359 *conventicle.* A meeting of Nonconformists, religious Dissenters: the
opprobrium attaching to the term was a consequence of the outlawing
of such meetings at the Restoration, though by 1700 they were no longer
illegal. Puritan sects were notorious for their singing (at least among non-
Puritans).

BETTY

They are gone sir, in great anger.

PETULANT

Enough, let 'em trundle. Anger helps complexion, saves paint.

FAINALL

This continence is all dissembled; this is in order to have something to brag of the next time he makes court to 370 Millamant, and swear he has abandoned the whole sex for her sake.

MIRABELL

Have you not left off your impudent pretensions there yet? I shall cut your throat sometime or other, Petulant, about that business. 375

PETULANT

Ay, ay, let that pass; there are other throats to be cut—

MIRABELL

Meaning mine, sir?

PETULANT

Not I—I mean nobody—I know nothing—but there are uncles and nephews in the world—and they may be rivals— what then? All's one for that— 380

MIRABELL

How! Harkee, Petulant, come hither. Explain, or I shall call your interpreter.

PETULANT

Explain? I know nothing. Why, you have an uncle, have you not, lately come to town, and lodges by my Lady Wishfort's?

MIRABELL

True. 385

PETULANT

Why, that's enough. You and he are not friends; and if he should marry and have a child, you may be disinherited, ha?

MIRABELL

Where hast thou stumbled upon all this truth?

PETULANT

All's one for that. Why then, say I know something.

367 *trundle* slang: 'make off'
376 *let that pass* . . . cf. *Henry V*, II, i, 20–25: 'I cannot tell; things must be as they may. Men may sleep, and they may have their throats about them at that time; and some say knives have edges. It must be as it may; though patience be a tired mare, yet she will plod. There must be conclusions. Well, I cannot tell.'

MIRABELL

Come, thou art an honest fellow, Petulant, and shalt make   390
love to my mistress, thou shalt i'faith. What hast thou heard
of my uncle?

PETULANT

I? Nothing, I. If throats are to be cut, let swords clash; snug's
the word; I shrug and am silent.

MIRABELL

Oh raillery, raillery. Come, I know thou art in the women's   395
secrets. What, you're a cabalist. I know you stayed at Millamant's last night, after I went. Was there any mention made
of my uncle, or me? Tell me. If thou hadst but good nature
equal to thy wit, Petulant, Tony Witwoud, who is now thy
competitor in fame, would show as dim by thee as a dead   400
whiting's eye by a pearl of orient. He would no more be seen
by thee, than Mercury is by the sun. Come, I'm sure thou
wilt tell me.

PETULANT

If I do, will you grant me commonsense then for the future.

MIRABELL

Faith I'll do what I can for thee; and I'll pray that heaven   405
may grant it thee in the meantime.

PETULANT

Well, harkee.

FAINALL

Petulant and you both will find Mirabell as warm a rival as a
lover.

WITWOUD

Pshaw, pshaw! That she laughs at Petulant is plain; and for   410
my part—but that it is almost a fashion to admire her, I
should—harkee—to tell you a secret, but let it go no further
—between friends, I shall never break my heart for her.

FAINALL

How!

WITWOUD

She's handsome; but she's a sort of an uncertain woman.   415

403 *wilt* ed. (wo't Q1, Q2, Ww)

---

401 *whiting's eye.* The whiting has pearly white flesh; its dead eye would be
dull and glazed; and there may be a play upon the proverbial meaning of
whiting's eye = amorous leer.
401 *pearl of orient* brilliant and precious pearls, as distinct from those found
in European waters, which are dull

FAINALL

I thought you had died for her.

WITWOUD

Umh—no—

FAINALL

She has wit.

WITWOUD

'Tis what she will hardly allow anybody else. Now, demme,
I should hate that, if she were as handsome as Cleopatra.   420
Mirabell is not so sure of her as he thinks for.

FAINALL

Why do you think so?

WITWOUD

We stayed pretty late there last night, and heard something
of an uncle to Mirabell who is lately come to town, and is
between him and the best part of his estate. Mirabell and he   425
are at some distance, as my Lady Wishfort has been told;
and you know she hates Mirabell worse than a quaker hates
a parrot, or than a fishmonger hates a hard frost. Whether
this uncle has seen Mrs. Millamant or not, I cannot say; but
there were items of such a treaty being in embryo; and if it   430
should come to life, poor Mirabell would be in some sort
unfortunately fobbed, i'faith.

FAINALL

'Tis impossible Millamant should hearken to it.

WITWOUD

Faith, my dear, I can't tell; she's a woman and a kind of a
humorist.   435

MIRABELL

And this is the sum of what you could collect last night.

PETULANT

The quintessence. Maybe Witwoud knows more, he stayed
longer; besides, they never mind him; they say anything
before him.

MIRABELL

I thought you had been the greatest favourite.   440

427-8 *worse than a quaker hates a parrot.* A quaker's pacific principles and
     plain dress and manners contrast with the gaudy plumage and chatter
     of a parrot.
428 *a fishmonger hates a hard frost* because ice makes fishing impossible
432 *fobbed*, tricked, cheated
435 *humorist* capricious person

PETULANT

Ay, *tête à tête*; but not in public, because I make remarks.

MIRABELL

Do you?

PETULANT

Ay, ay, pox, I'm malicious, man. Now he's soft you know, they are not in awe of him—the fellow's well-bred, he's what you call a—what-d'ye-call-'em—a fine gentleman; but he's 445 silly withal.

MIRABELL

I thank you, I know as much as my curiosity requires. Fainall, are you for the Mall?

FAINALL

Ay, I'll take a turn before dinner.

WITWOUD

Ay, we'll all walk in the park; the ladies talked of being 450 there.

MIRABELL

I thought you were obliged to watch for your brother Sir Wilfull's arrival.

WITWOUD

No, no, he comes to his aunt's, my Lady Wishfort; pox on him, I shall be troubled with him too; what shall I do with 455 the fool?

PETULANT

Beg him for his estate, that I may beg you afterwards, and so have but one trouble with you both.

WITWOUD

Oh rare Petulant! Thou art as quick as a fire in a frosty morning; thou shalt to the Mall with us; and we'll be very 460 severe.

PETULANT

Enough. I'm in a humour to be severe.

MIRABELL

Are you? Pray then walk by yourselves—let not us be accessory to your putting the ladies out of countenance with your senseless ribaldry, which you roar out aloud as often as 465

441 *tête à tête* ed. (teste a teste Q1, Q2)
442 *Do you?* Q1, Q2 (You do? Ww)
459 *a fire* Q1, Q2 (fire Ww)

448 *the Mall*. A gravel walk bordered by trees in St James's Park, originally the alley in which the game of mall was played, later a fashionable promenade. Etherege sets II, iii, of *The Man of Mode* in the Mall.

they pass by you; and when you have made a handsome
woman blush, then you think you have been severe.

PETULANT

What, what? Then let 'em either show their innocence by not
understanding what they hear, or else show their discretion
by not hearing what they would not be thought to under-   470
stand.

MIRABELL

But hast not thou then sense enough to know that thou
ought'st to be most ashamed thyself, when thou hast put
another out of countenance?

PETULANT

Not I, by this hand; I always take blushing either for a sign   475
of guilt, or ill-breeding.

MIRABELL

I confess you ought to think so. You are in the right, that
you may plead the error of your judgement in defence of your
practice.

> Where modesty's ill manners, 'tis but fit   480
> That impudence and malice pass for wit.   *Exeunt*

Act II, Scene i

St. James's Park
Enter MRS. FAINALL *and* MRS. MARWOOD

MRS. FAINALL

Ay, ay, dear Marwood, if we will be happy, we must find the
means in ourselves, and among ourselves. Men are ever in ex-
tremes, either doting or averse. While they are lovers, if
they have fire and sense their jealousies are insupportable;
and when they cease to love (we ought to think at least) they   5
loathe. They look upon us with horror and distaste; they meet
us like the ghosts of what we were, and as such fly from us.

MRS. MARWOOD

True, 'tis an unhappy circumstance of life, that love should
ever die before us, and that the man so often should outlive
the lover. But say what you will, 'tis better to be left than   10
never to have been loved. To pass our youth in dull indifference, to refuse the sweets of life because they once must leave
us, is as preposterous as to wish to have been born old,
because we one day must be old. For my part, my youth
may wear and waste, but it shall never rust in my possession.   15

7 *as such* Q1, Q2 (as from such Ww)

3   *   *

MRS. FAINALL

Then it seems you dissemble an aversion to mankind only in
compliance with my mother's humour.

MRS. MARWOOD

Certainly—to be free. I have no taste of those insipid dry
discourses with which our sex, of force, must entertain themselves apart from men. We may affect endearments to each   20
other, profess eternal friendships, and seem to dote like
lovers; but 'tis not in our natures long to persevere. Love
will resume his empire in our breasts, and every heart, or
soon, or late, receive and readmit him as its lawful tyrant.

MRS. FAINALL

Bless me, how have I been deceived! Why, you profess a   25
libertine!

MRS. MARWOOD

You see my friendship by my freedom. Come, be as sincere;
acknowledge that your sentiments agree with mine.

MRS. FAINALL

Never.

MRS. MARWOOD

You hate mankind.   30

MRS. FAINALL

Heartily, inveterately.

MRS. MARWOOD

Your husband.

MRS. FAINALL

Most transcendently! Ay, though I say it, meritoriously.

MRS. MARWOOD

Give me your hand upon it.

MRS. FAINALL

There.   35

MRS. MARWOOD

I join with you; what I have said has been to try you.

MRS. FAINALL

Is it possible? Dost thou hate those vipers, men?

MRS. MARWOOD

I have done hating 'em, and am now come to despise 'em;
the next thing I have to do, is eternally to forget 'em.

MRS. FAINALL

There spoke the spirit of an Amazon, a Penthesilea.   40

17 *compliance with* Q1, Q2 (compliance to Ww)

---

19 *of force* of necessity
40 *Penthesilea* Amazonian queen

MRS. MARWOOD

And yet I am thinking, sometimes, to carry my aversion
further.

MRS. FAINALL

How?

MRS. MARWOOD

Faith, by marrying; if I could but find one that loved me very
well, and would be thoroughly sensible of ill usage, I think I   45
should do myself the violence of undergoing the ceremony.

MRS. FAINALL

You would not make him a cuckold?

MRS. MARWOOD

No; but I'd make him believe I did, and that's as bad.

MRS. FAINALL

Why, had not you as good do it?

MRS. MARWOOD

Oh if he should ever discover it, he would then know the   50
worst, and be out of his pain; but I would have him ever to
continue upon the rack of fear and jealousy.

MRS. FAINALL

Ingenious mischief! Would thou wert married to Mirabell.

MRS. MARWOOD

Would I were.

MRS. FAINALL

You change colour.   55

MRS. MARWOOD

Because I hate him.

MRS. FAINALL

So do I; but I can hear him named. But what reason have you
to hate him in particular?

MRS. MARWOOD

I never loved him; he is, and always was insufferably proud.

MRS. FAINALL

By the reason you give for your aversion, one would think   60
it dissembled; for you have laid a fault to his charge of which
his enemies must acquit him.

MRS. MARWOOD

Oh, then it seems you are one of his favourable enemies.
Methinks you look a little pale—and now you flush again.

MRS. FAINALL

Do I? I think I am a little sick o' the sudden.   65

MRS. MARWOOD

What ails you?

MRS. FAINALL

My husband; don't you see him? He turned short upon me
unawares and has almost overcome me.

Enter FAINALL *and* MIRABELL

MRS. MARWOOD

Ha, ha, ha! He comes opportunely for you.

MRS. FAINALL

For you, for he has brought Mirabell with him.   70

FAINALL

My dear.

MRS. FAINALL

My soul.

FAINALL

You don't look well today, child.

MRS. FAINALL

D'ye think so?

MIRABELL

He is the only man that does, madam.   75

MRS. FAINALL

The only man that would tell me so, at least; and the only
man from whom I could hear it without mortification.

FAINALL

Oh, my dear, I am satisfied of your tenderness; I know you
cannot resent anything from me, especially what is an effect
of my concern.   80

MRS. FAINALL

Mr. Mirabell, my mother interrupted you in a pleasant relation last night; I would fain hear it out.

MIRABELL

The persons concerned in that affair have yet a tolerable
reputation; I am afraid Mr. Fainall will be censorious.

MRS. FAINALL

He has a humour more prevailing than his curiosity, and will   85
willingly dispense with the hearing of one scandalous story,
to avoid giving an occasion to make another by being seen to
walk with his wife. This way Mr. Mirabell, and I dare
promise you will oblige us both.

Exeunt MRS. FAINALL *and* MIRABELL

FAINALL

Excellent creature! Well sure if I should live to be rid of my   90
wife, I should be a miserable man.

MRS. MARWOOD

Ay!

FAINALL

For having only that one hope, the accomplishment of it of
consequence must put an end to all my hopes; and what a
wretch is he who must survive his hopes! Nothing remains   95
when that day comes, but to sit down and weep like
Alexander, when he wanted other worlds to conquer.

MRS. MARWOOD

Will you not follow 'em?

FAINALL

Faith, I think not.

MRS. MARWOOD

Pray let us; I have a reason.   100

FAINALL

You are not jealous?

MRS. MARWOOD

Of whom?

FAINALL

Of Mirabell.

MRS. MARWOOD

If I am, is it inconsistent with my love to you that I am
tender of your honour?   105

FAINALL

You would intimate then, as if there were a fellow-feeling
between my wife and him.

MRS. MARWOOD

I think she does not hate him to that degree she would be
thought.

FAINALL

But he, I fear, is too insensible.   110

MRS. MARWOOD

It may be you are deceived.

FAINALL

It may be so. I do not now begin to apprehend it.

MRS. MARWOOD

What?

FAINALL

That I have been deceived, madam, and you are false.

112 *I do not now* ed. (I do now Q1)

97 *Alexander* reminiscent of Molière, *Dom Juan*, when Juan declares his
libertine philosophy: 'Il n'est rien qui puisse arrêter l'impétuosité de
mes désirs: je me sens un coeur à aimer toute la terre; et comme Alex-
andre, je souhaiterais qu'il y eût d'autres mondes, pour y pouvoir
étendre mes conquêtes amoureuses.' (I, ii).

MRS. MARWOOD

That I am false! What mean you?   115

FAINALL

To let you know I see through all your little arts. Come, you
both love him; and both have equally dissembled your
aversion. Your mutual jealousies of one another have made
you clash till you have both struck fire. I have seen the warm
confession reddening on your cheeks and sparkling from   120
your eyes.

MRS. MARWOOD

You do me wrong.

FAINALL

I do not. 'Twas for my ease to oversee and wilfully neglect
the gross advances made him by my wife; that by permitting
her to be engaged, I might continue unsuspected in my   125
pleasures, and take you oftener to my arms in full security.
But could you think, because the nodding husband would not
wake, that e'er the watchful lover slept?

MRS. MARWOOD

And wherewithal can you reproach me?

FAINALL

With infidelity, with loving of another, with love of Mirabell.   130

MRS. MARWOOD

'Tis false. I challenge you to show an instance that can
confirm your groundless accusation. I hate him.

FAINALL

And wherefore do you hate him? He is insensible, and your
resentment follows his neglect. An instance? The injuries
you have done him are a proof: your interposing in his love.   135
What cause had you to make discoveries of his pretended
passion? To undeceive the credulous aunt, and be the
officious obstacle of his match with Millamant.

MRS. MARWOOD

My obligations to my lady urged me. I had professed a
friendship to her, and could not see her easy nature so abused   140
by that dissembler.

FAINALL

What! Was it conscience then! Professed a friendship! Oh
the pious friendships of the female sex!

MRS. MARWOOD

More tender, more sincere, and more enduring, than all the

130 *loving of another* Q1, Q2 (loving another Ww)

vain and empty vows of men, whether professing love to us,   145
or mutual faith to one another.

FAINALL

Ha, ha, ha! You are my wife's friend too.

MRS. MARWOOD

Shame and ingratitude! Do you reproach me? You, you,
upbraid me? Have I been false to her through strict fidelity
to you, and sacrificed my friendship to keep my love inviolate,   150
and have you the baseness to charge me with the guilt,
unmindful of the merit! To you it should be meritorious that
I have been vicious: and do you reflect that guilt upon me,
which should lie buried in your bosom?

FAINALL

You misinterpret my reproof. I meant but to remind you of   155
the slight account you once could make of strictest ties, when
set in competition with your love to me.

MRS. MARWOOD

'Tis false, you urged it with deliberate malice—'twas spoke
in scorn, and I never will forgive it.

FAINALL

Your guilt, not your resentment, begets your rage. If yet   160
you loved, you could forgive a jealousy; but you are stung to
find you are discovered.

MRS. MARWOOD

It shall be all discovered—you too shall be discovered! Be
sure you shall! I can but be exposed; if I do it myself I shall
prevent your baseness.   165

FAINALL

Why, what will you do?

MRS. MARWOOD

Disclose it to your wife; own what has passed between us.

FAINALL

Frenzy!

MRS. MARWOOD

By all my wrongs, I'll do't! I'll publish to the world the
injuries you have done me, both in my fame and fortune: 170
with both I trusted you, you—bankrupt in honour, as indi-
gent of wealth!

FAINALL

Your fame I have preserved; your fortune has been bestowed
as the prodigality of your love would have it, in pleasures

157 *competition* Q1-Ww (comparison *Lynch*)

---

165 *prevent* anticipate

which we both have shared. Yet had not you been false, I had   175
ere this repaid it. 'Tis true! Had you permitted Mirabell with
Millamant to have stolen their marriage, my lady had been
incensed beyond all means of reconcilement. Millamant
had forfeited the moiety of her fortune, which then would
have descended to my wife; and wherefore did I marry, but   180
to make lawful prize of a rich widow's wealth, and squander
it on love and you?

MRS. MARWOOD

Deceit and frivolous pretence!

FAINALL

Death, am I not married? What's pretence? Am I not
imprisoned, fettered? Have I not a wife? Nay, a wife that   185
was a widow, a young widow, a handsome widow; and
would be again a widow, but that I have a heart of proof
and something of a constitution, to bustle through the ways
of wedlock and this world. Will you yet be reconciled to
truth and me?   190

MRS. MARWOOD

Impossible; truth and you are inconsistent! I hate you, and
shall for ever.

FAINALL

For loving you?

MRS. MARWOOD

I loathe the name of love, after such usage; and next to the
guilt with which you would asperse me, I scorn you most.   195
Farewell.

FAINALL

Nay, we must not part thus.

MRS. MARWOOD

Let me go!

FAINALL

Come, I'm sorry.

MRS. MARWOOD

I care not—let me go—break my hands, do! I'd leave 'em   200
to get loose.

FAINALL

I would not hurt you for the world. Have I no other hold to
keep you here?

MRS. MARWOOD

Well, I have deserved it all.

179 *moiety* half
188 *bustle* possibly reminiscent of *Richard III*, I, i, 152

FAINALL

You know I love you.   205

MRS. MARWOOD

Poor dissembling—oh that—well, it is not yet—

FAINALL

What? What is it not? What is it not yet? It is not yet too
late—

MRS. MARWOOD

No, it is not yet too late; I have that comfort.

FAINALL

It is, to love another.   210

MRS. MARWOOD

But not to loathe, detest, abhor mankind, myself, and the
whole treacherous world.

FAINALL

Nay, this is extravagance! Come, I ask your pardon—no
tears—I was to blame; I could not love you and be easy in my
doubts. Pray forbear—I believe you. I'm convinced I've   215
done you wrong, and any way, every way, will make amends.
I'll hate my wife yet more, damn her! I'll part with her, rob
her of all she's worth, and we'll retire somewhere, anywhere,
to another world—I'll marry thee—be pacified—'sdeath, they
come! Hide your face, your tears! You have a mask, wear it a 220
moment. This way, this way, be persuaded!   *Exeunt*

Enter MIRABELL *and* MRS. FAINALL

MRS. FAINALL

They are here yet.

MIRABELL

They are turning into the other walk.

MRS. FAINALL

While I only hated my husband, I could bear to see him; but
since I have despised him, he's too offensive.   225

MIRABELL

Oh you should hate with prudence.

MRS. FAINALL

Yes, for I have loved with indiscretion.

MIRABELL

You should have just so much disgust for your husband as
may be sufficient to make you relish your lover.

215–16 *I've done* Q1 (I have done Q2, Ww)
218 *we'll retire* ed. (will retire Q1, Q2)

MRS. FAINALL

You have been the cause that I have loved without bounds,   230
and would you set limits to that aversion of which you have
been the occasion? Why did you make me marry this man?

MIRABELL

Why do we daily commit disagreeable and dangerous
actions? To save that idol, reputation. If the familiarities of
our loves had produced that consequence, of which you were   235
apprehensive, where could you have fixed a father's name
with credit, but on a husband? I knew Fainall to be a man
lavish of his morals: an interested and professing friend, a
false and a designing lover; yet one whose wit and outward
fair behaviour have gained a reputation with the town,   240
enough to make that woman stand excused, who has suffered
herself to be won by his address. A better man ought not to
have been sacrificed to the occasion; a worse had not
answered to the purpose. When you are weary of him, you
know your remedy.   245

MRS. FAINALL

I ought to stand in some degree of credit with you, Mirabell.

MIRABELL

In justice to you, I have made you privy to my whole design,
and put it in your power to ruin or advance my fortune.

MRS. FAINALL

Whom have you instructed to represent your pretended
uncle?   250

MIRABELL

Waitwell, my servant.

MRS. FAINALL

He is an humble servant to Foible, my mother's woman, and
may win her to your interest.

MIRABELL

Care is taken for that—she is won and worn by this time.
They were married this morning.   255

MRS. FAINALL

Who?

MIRABELL

Waitwell and Foible. I would not tempt my servant to betray
me by trusting him too far. If your mother, in hopes to ruin
me, should consent to marry my pretended uncle, he might,

238 *lavish* licentious

like Mosca in *The Fox*, stand upon terms; so I made him sure   260
beforehand.

MRS. FAINALL

So, if my poor mother is caught in a contract, you will discover the imposture betimes and release her, by producing
a certificate of her gallant's former marriage.

MIRABELL

Yes, upon condition she consent to my marriage with her   265
niece and surrender the moiety of her fortune in her possession.

MRS. FAINALL

She talked last night of endeavouring at a match between
Millamant and your uncle.

MIRABELL

That was by Foible's direction, and my instruction, that she   270
might seem to carry it more privately.

MRS. FAINALL

Well, I have an opinion of your success, for I believe my lady
will do anything to get a husband, and when she has this
which you have provided for her, I suppose she will submit
to anything to get rid of him.   275

MIRABELL

Yes, I think the good lady would marry anything that
resembled a man, though 'twere no more than what a butler
could pinch out of a napkin.

MRS. FAINALL

Female frailty! We must all come to it, if we live to be old,
and feel the craving of a false appetite when the true is   280
decayed.

MIRABELL

An old woman's appetite is depraved like that of a girl—'tis
the green sickness of a second childhood; and like the faint
offer of a latter Spring, serves but to usher in the Fall, and
withers in an affected bloom.   285

MRS. FAINALL

Here's your mistress.

Enter MRS. MILLAMANT, WITWOUD *and* MINCING

---

265 *condition she* Q1, Q2 (condition that she Ww)

---

260 *Mosca in The Fox.* In *Volpone* Mosca the parasite-servant refuses to
deliver Volpone from judgement even when Volpone offers him half the
spoils. Mosca wants all, and the result is that both he and Volpone fall
(*Volpone*, V, xii).
284 *latter Spring.* Falstaff is called this by Prince Hal in *1 Henry IV*, I, ii, 152.

MIRABELL

Here she comes i'faith full sail, with her fan spread and her
streamers out, and a shoal of fools for tenders—ha, no, I cry
her mercy.

MRS. FAINALL

I see but one poor empty sculler, and he tows her woman   290
after him.

MIRABELL

You seem to be unattended, madam. You used to have the
beau monde throng after you, and a flock of gay fine perukes
hovering round you.

WITWOUD

Like moths about a candle. I had like to have lost my   295
comparison for want of breath!

MILLAMANT

Oh I have denied myself airs today. I have walked as fast
through the crowd—

WITWOUD

As a favourite in disgrace; and with as few followers.

MILLAMANT

Dear Mr. Witwoud, truce with your similitudes; for I am as   300
sick of 'em—

WITWOUD

As a physician of a good air—I cannot help it madam, though
'tis against myself.

MILLAMANT

Yet again! Mincing, stand between me and his wit.

WITWOUD

Do Mrs. Mincing, like a screen before a great fire. I confess   305
I do blaze today, I am too bright.

MRS. FAINALL

But dear Millamant, why were you so long?

MILLAMANT

Long! Lord, have I not made violent haste? I have asked
every living thing I met for you; I have enquired after you
as after a new fashion.   310

287–8 *her streamers* Q1, Q2 (streamers Ww)
299 *in disgrace* Q1, Q2 (just disgraced Ww)

---

288 *streamers* ribbons, suggesting a flag-bedecked ship dressed overall and
    entering port; Dryden, *An Evening's Love*, II, i, has Wildblood mark-
    ing Jacinta's entrance with 'Yonder she comes with full sails i'faith; I'll
    hail her amain for England.'
290 *sculler* a small boat rowed by a single oarsman
293 *peruke* wig

WITWOUD

Madam, truce with your similitudes! No, you met her husband and did not ask him for her.

MIRABELL

By your leave Witwoud, that were like enquiring after an old fashion, to ask a husband for his wife.

WITWOUD

Hum; a hit, a hit, a palpable hit, I confess it.   315

MRS. FAINALL

You were dressed before I came abroad.

MILLAMANT

Ay, that's true—oh but then I had—Mincing what had I? Why was I so long?

MINCING

Oh mem, your la'ship stayed to peruse a pecquet of letters.

MILLAMANT

Oh ay, letters—I had letters—I am persecuted with letters—   320
I hate letters—nobody knows how to write letters; and yet one has 'em, one does not know why. They serve one to pin up one's hair.

WITWOUD

Is that the way? Pray madam, do you pin up your hair with all your letters? I find I must keep copies.   325

MILLAMANT

Only with those in verse, Mr. Witwoud, I never pin up my hair with prose. I fancy one's hair would not curl if it were pinned up with prose. I think I tried once Mincing?

MINCING

Oh mem, I shall never forget it.

MILLAMANT

Ay, poor Mincing tift and tift all the morning.   330

MINCING

Till I had the cremp in my fingers I'll vow mem, and all to no purpose. But when your la'ship pins it up with poetry, it sits so pleasant the next day as anything and is so pure and so crips.

---

319 *pecquet* Q1 (pacquet Q2, Ww)
327–8 *I fancy . . . prose* Q1 (omitted Q2, Ww)
331 *cremp* Q1 (cramp Q2, Ww)

---

319 *pecquet* Mincing speaks affectedly.
330 *tift*. A usage in 1600 of this rare verb has the past perfect form 'tifted' (OED); it means 'prepare', 'make ready'.
334 *crips* obsolete form of 'crisp'

WITWOUD

Indeed, so crips?   335

MINCING

You're such a critic, Mr. Witwoud.

MILLAMANT

Mirabell, did not you take exceptions last night? Oh ay, and
went away—now I think on't I'm angry—no, now I think
on't I'm pleased—for I believe I gave you some pain.

MIRABELL

Does that please you?   340

MILLAMANT

Infinitely; I love to give pain.

MIRABELL

You would affect a cruelty which is not in your nature;
your true vanity is in the power of pleasing.

MILLAMANT

Oh I ask your pardon for that—one's cruelty is one's
power, and when one parts with one's cruelty one parts with   345
one's power; and when one has parted with that, I fancy
one's old and ugly.

MIRABELL

Ay, ay, suffer your cruelty to ruin the object of your power,
to destroy your lover—and then how vain, how lost a thing
you'll be! Nay, 'tis true; you are no longer handsome when   350
you've lost your lover. Your beauty dies upon the instant; for
beauty is the lover's gift; 'tis he bestows your charms: your
glass is all a cheat. The ugly and the old, whom the looking-
glass mortifies, yet after commendation can be flattered by it
and discover beauties in it; for that reflects our praises rather 355
than your face.

MILLAMANT

Oh the vanity of these men! Fainall, d'ye hear him? If they
did not commend us, we were not handsome! Now you must
know they could not commend one, if one was not handsome.
Beauty the lover's gift! Lord, what is a lover, that it can give?   360
Why, one makes lovers as fast as one pleases, and they live
as long as one pleases, and they die as soon as one pleases;
and then, if one pleases, one makes more.

WITWOUD

Very pretty. Why, you make no more of making of lovers,
madam, than of making so many card-matches.   365

337 *did not* Q1, Q2 (did Ww)

---

365 *card-matches* matches made from cardboard

MILLAMANT

One no more owes one's beauty to a lover, than one's wit to an echo; they can but reflect what we look and say: vain empty things if we are silent or unseen, and want a being.

MIRABELL

Yet to those two vain empty things you owe two of the greatest pleasures of your life.   370

MILLAMANT

How so?

MIRABELL

To your lover you owe the pleasure of hearing yourselves praised, and to an echo the pleasure of hearing yourselves talk.

WITWOUD

But I know a lady that loves talking so incessantly she won't   375
give an echo fair play; she has that everlasting rotation of tongue, that an echo must wait till she dies before it can catch her last words.

MILLAMANT

Oh fiction! Fainall, let us leave these men.

MIRABELL (*Aside to* MRS. FAINALL)

Draw off Witwoud.   380

MRS. FAINALL

Immediately; I have a word or two for Mr. Witwoud.

MIRABELL

I would beg a little private audience too—

Exeunt WITWOUD *and* MRS. FAINALL

You had the tyranny to deny me last night, though you knew I came to impart a secret to you that concerned my love.

MILLAMANT

You saw I was engaged.   385

MIRABELL

Unkind. You had the leisure to entertain a herd of fools— things who visit you from their excessive idleness, bestowing on your easiness that time which is the incumbrance of their lives. How can you find delight in such society? It is impossible they should admire you, they are not capable; or if they   390
were, it should be to you as a mortification: so sure to please a fool is some degree of folly.

MILLAMANT

I please myself; besides, sometimes to converse with fools is for my health.

MIRABELL

Your health! Is there a worse disease than the conversation   395
of fools?

MILLAMANT

Yes, the vapours; fools are physic for it next to assafoetida.

MIRABELL

You are not in a course of fools?

MILLAMANT

Mirabell, if you persist in this offensive freedom, you'll
displease me. I think I must resolve after all not to have   400
you—we shan't agree.

MIRABELL

Not in our physic, it may be.

MILLAMANT

And yet our distemper in all likelihood will be the same; for
we shall be sick of one another. I shan't endure to be repri-
manded nor instructed; 'tis so dull to act always by advice,   405
and so tedious to be told of one's faults: I can't bear it. Well,
I won't have you, Mirabell. I'm resolved—I think—you may
go. Ha, ha, ha! What would you give, that you could help
loving me?

MIRABELL

I would give something that you did not know I could not   410
help it.

MILLAMANT

Come, don't look grave then. Well, what do you say to me?

MIRABELL

I say that a man may as soon make a friend by his wit, or a
fortune by his honesty, as win a woman with plain dealing
and sincerity.   415

MILLAMANT

Sententious Mirabell! Prithee don't look with that violent
and inflexible wise face, like Solomon at the dividing of the
child in an old tapestry hanging.

MIRABELL

You are merry, madam, but I would persuade you for one
moment to be serious.   420

419–20 *one moment* Q1, Q2, W1 (a moment W2)

---

397 *assafoetida* a resinous gum with a strong alliacious odour, procured in
  Central Asia; used as an antispasmodic (OED)
398 *course of fools.* The company of fools is supposedly medicinal.
417 *Solomon* the episode of I Kings 3

MILLAMANT

What, with that face? No, if you keep your countenance, 'tis impossible I should hold mine. Well, after all, there is something very moving in a love-sick face—ha, ha, ha!—well I won't laugh; don't be peevish. Heigh-ho! Now I'll be melancholy, as melancholy as a watch-light. Well, Mirabell, if 425 ever you will win me, woo me now. Nay, if you are so tedious, fare you well; I see they are walking away.

MIRABELL

Can you not find in the variety of your disposition one moment—

MILLAMANT

To hear you tell me that Foible's married, and your plot 430 like to speed? No.

MIRABELL

But how you came to know it—

MILLAMANT

Unless by the help of the devil, you can't imagine, unless she should tell me herself. Which of the two it may have been, I will leave you to consider; and when you have done thinking 435 of that, think of me.   *Exit*

MIRABELL

I have something more—gone! Think of you! To think of a whirlwind, though 'twere in a whirlwind, were a case of more steady contemplation: a very tranquillity of mind and mansion. A fellow that lives in a windmill has not a more 440 whimsical dwelling than the heart of a man that is lodged in a woman. There is no point of the compass to which they cannot turn, and by which they are not turned; and by one as well as another; for motion, not method, is their occupation. To know this, and yet continue to be in love, is to be made 445 wise from the dictates of reason, and yet persevere to play the fool by the force of instinct. Oh here come my pair of turtles—what, billing so sweetly! Is not Valentine's Day over with you yet?

Enter WAITWELL *and* FOIBLE

Sirrah, Waitwell, why sure you think you were married for 450 your own recreation, and not for my conveniency.

---

430 *that Foible's* Q1 (Foible's Q2, Ww)
433 *Unless by the help* Q1, Q2 (without the help Ww)

---

425 *watch-light* night-light

WAITWELL

Your pardon, sir. With submission, we have indeed been solacing in lawful delights; but still with an eye to business, sir. I have instructed her as well as I could. If she can take your directions as readily as my instructions, sir, your affairs   455
are in a prosperous way.

MIRABELL

Give you joy, Mrs. Foible.

FOIBLE

Oh 'las sir, I'm so ashamed—I'm afraid my lady has been in a thousand inquietudes for me. But I protest, sir, I made as much haste as I could.   460

WAITWELL

That she did indeed, sir. It was my fault that she did not make more.

MIRABELL

That I believe.

FOIBLE

But I told my lady as you instructed me, sir, that I had a prospect of seeing Sir Rowland your uncle, and that I would   465
put her ladyship's picture in my pocket to show him; which I'll be sure to say has made him so enamoured of her beauty, that he burns with impatience to lie at her ladyship's feet and worship the original.

MIRABELL

Excellent Foible! Matrimony has made you eloquent in love.   470

WAITWELL

I think she has profited, sir; I think so.

FOIBLE

You have seen Madam Millamant, sir?

MIRABELL

Yes.

FOIBLE

I told her, sir, because I did not know that you might find an opportunity; she had so much company last night.   475

MIRABELL

Your diligence will merit more—in the mean time—(*gives money*)

FOIBLE

Oh dear sir, your humble servant.

WAITWELL

Spouse.

471 *profited*. Waitwell parodies Puritan jargon.

MIRABELL

Stand off sir, not a penny—go on, and prosper, Foible; the
lease shall be made good and the farm stocked, if we   480
succeed.

FOIBLE

I don't question your generosity, sir; and you need not doubt
of success. If you have no more commands sir, I'll be gone.
I'm sure my lady is at her toilet, and can't dress till I come.
Oh dear (*looking out*) I'm sure that was Mrs. Marwood that   485
went by in a mask; if she has seen me with you I'm sure she'll
tell my lady. I'll make haste home and prevent her. Your
servant sir. B'w'y, Waitwell.   *Exit* FOIBLE

WAITWELL

Sir Rowland if you please. The jade's so pert upon her
preferment she forgets herself.   490

MIRABELL

Come sir, will you endeavour to forget yourself, and trans-
form into Sir Rowland.

WAITWELL

Why sir, it will be impossible I should remember myself—
married, knighted and attended all in one day! 'Tis enough
to make any man forget himself. The difficulty will be how to   495
recover my acquaintance and familiarity with my former self,
and fall from my transformation to a reformation into
Waitwell. Nay, I shan't be quite the same Waitwell neither—
for now I remember me, I am married, and can't be my
own man again.   500

> Ay there's the grief; that's the sad change of life;
> To lose my title and yet keep my wife.   *Exeunt*

Act III, Scene i

A room in LADY WISHFORT'*s house*
LADY WISHFORT *at her toilet*, PEG *waiting*

LADY WISHFORT

Merciful, no news of Foible yet?

PEG

No madam.

---

499 *I am married* Q1 (I'm married Q2, Ww)

---

488 *B'w'y* God be with you
490 *preferment* promotion

LADY WISHFORT

I have no more patience. If I have not fretted myself till I am
pale again, there's no veracity in me. Fetch me the red—the
red, do you hear, sweetheart! An arrant ash colour, as I'm a   5
person! Look you how this wench stirs! Why dost thou
not fetch me a little red? Didst thou not hear me, Mopus?

PEG

The red ratafia does your ladyship mean, or the cherry
brandy?

LADY WISHFORT

Ratafia, fool! No, fool! Not the ratafia, fool—grant me   10
patience! I mean the Spanish paper, idiot! Complexion,
darling. Paint, paint, paint! Dost thou understand that,
changeling? Dangling thy hands like bobbins before thee!
Why dost thou not stir, puppet? Thou wooden thing upon
wires.   15

PEG

Lord, madam, your ladyship is so impatient. I cannot come
at the paint, madam; Mrs. Foible has locked it up, and
carried the key with her.

LADY WISHFORT

A pox take you both! Fetch me the cherry brandy then.

Exit PEG

I'm as pale and as faint, I look like Mrs. Qualmsick the   20
curate's wife, that's always breeding. Wench, come, come,
wench, what art thou doing, sipping? Tasting? Save thee,
dost thou not know the bottle?

Enter PEG *with a bottle and china cup*

PEG

Madam, I was looking for a cup.

LADY WISHFORT

A cup! Save thee, and what a cup hast thou brought! Dost   25
thou take me for a fairy, to drink out of an acorn? Why didst
thou not bring thy thimble? Hast thou ne'er a brass thimble
clinking in thy pocket with a bit of nutmeg? I warrant thee.

7 *Mopus* dull, stupid person   11 *Spanish paper* rouge
13 *changeling* an ugly or stupid child supposedly left by fairies in exchange
for one stolen
27–8 *thimble . . . nutmeg* probably good-luck charms, but Swift, *Polite
Conversation*, has Miss searching in her pocket for a thimble, and bringing out a nutmeg, which provokes the comment 'O Miss, have a care; for
if you carry a Nutmeg in your Pocket, you'll certainly be married to an
old Man'. (Ed. H. Davis and L. Landa [Oxford, 1957], p. 163.)

Come, fill, fill. So. Again. (*one knocks*) See who that is. Set
down the bottle first. Here, here, under the table! What,   30
wouldst thou go with the bottle in thy hand like a tapster? As
I'm a person, this wench has lived in an inn upon the road
before she came to me, like Maritornes the Asturian in *Don
Quixote*. No Foible yet?

PEG

No madam; Mrs. Marwood.   35

LADY WISHFORT

Oh Marwood; let her come in. Come in, good Marwood.

Enter MRS. MARWOOD

MRS. MARWOOD

I'm surprised to find your ladyship in *déshabille* at this time
of day.

LADY WISHFORT

Foible's a lost thing; has been abroad since morning, and
never heard of since.   40

MRS. MARWOOD

I saw her but now, as I came masked through the park, in
conference with Mirabell.

LADY WISHFORT

With Mirabell! You call my blood into my face with men-
tioning that traitor. She durst not have the confidence. I sent
her to negotiate an affair, in which if I'm detected I'm   45
undone. If that wheedling villain has wrought upon Foible
to detect me, I'm ruined. Oh my dear friend, I'm a wretch of
wretches if I'm detected.

MRS. MARWOOD

Oh madam, you cannot suspect Mrs. Foible's integrity.

LADY WISHFORT

Oh, he carries poison in his tongue that would corrupt   50
integrity itself. If she has given him an opportunity, she has
as good as put her integrity into his hands. Ah dear Marwood, what's integrity to an opportunity? Hark! I hear her.
Go, you thing, and send her in.

Exit PEG

37 *déshabille* ed. (dishabilie Q1)
54 *Go, you thing, and send her in* placed at the end of Lady Wishfort's
speech in Ww

33 *Maritornes* the innkeeper's daughter who takes part in the scene when
Quixote is made a knight. Davis suggests Lady Wishfort would remember D'Urfey's popular play, Pt I, II, i.

Dear friend retire into my closet, that I may examine her with   55
more freedom. You'll pardon me dear friend, I can make
bold with you—there are books over the chimney—
Quarles and Prynne, and the *Short View of the Stage*, with
Bunyan's works, to entertain you.

Exit MRS. MARWOOD

Enter FOIBLE

Oh Foible, where hast thou been? What hast thou been   60
doing?

FOIBLE

Madam, I have seen the party.

LADY WISHFORT

But what hast thou done?

FOIBLE

Nay, 'tis your ladyship has done, and are to do; I have only
promised. But a man so enamoured—so transported! Well,   65
here it is, all that is left ; [*shows picture*] all that is not kissed
away. Well, if worshipping of pictures be a sin—poor Sir
Rowland, I say.

LADY WISHFORT

The miniature has been counted like; but hast thou not
betrayed me, Foible? Hast thou not detected me to that   70
faithless Mirabell? What hadst thou to do with him in the
park? Answer me: has he got nothing out of thee?

FOIBLE

So, the devil has been beforehand with me; what shall I say?
[*Aside*] Alas, madam, could I help it, if I met that confident
thing? Was I in fault? If you had heard how he used me, and   75

65-7 *Well, here it is . . . kissed away* (omitted Q2, Ww)

58 *Quarles.* Francis Quarles (1592–1644), author of the popular *Emblems,
Divine and Moral* (1635) and of biblical narratives
58 *Prynne.* William Prynne wrote *Histrio-mastix*, a Puritan attack on the
stage, in 1632.
58 *Short View.* Jeremy Collier's attack on the immorality and profaneness
of the English stage came out two years before *The Way of the World*
and included attacks on Congreve's earlier comedies.
59 *Bunyan's Works. Grace Abounding* (1666), *Pilgrim's Progress* (1678–79),
The Life and Death of Mr Badman (1680), *The Holy War* (1682), reprinted frequently and very popular Puritan literature. Congreve
mocked Puritans and their literature in his first play *The Old Bachelor*,
where the merchant Fondlewife uses Puritan jargon and the gallant
mocks *The Practice of Piety.* Lady Wishfort's taste in literature is
suited to her view on the education of daughters, as expressed in Act V.

all upon your ladyship's account, I'm sure you would not
suspect my fidelity. Nay, if that had been the worst, I could
have borne; but he had a fling at your ladyship too—and then
I could not hold; but, i'faith, I gave him his own!

LADY WISHFORT

Me? What did the filthy fellow say?   80

FOIBLE

Oh madam, 'tis a shame to say what he said—with his taunts
and his fleers, tossing up his nose. Humh (says he), what, you
are a-hatching some plot (says he), you are so early abroad,
or catering (says he), ferreting, for some disbanded officer,
I warrant. Half-pay is but thin subsistence (says he). Well,   85
what pension does your lady propose? Let me see (says he),
what, she must come down pretty deep now, she's superannuated (says he), and—

LADY WISHFORT

Ods my life, I'll have him, I'll have him murdered! I'll have
him poisoned! Where does he eat? I'll marry a drawer to   90
have him poisoned in his wine. I'll send for Robin from
Locket's immediately.

FOIBLE

Poison him? Poisoning's too good for him. Starve him
madam, starve him—marry Sir Rowland and get him
disinherited! Oh you would bless yourself to hear what he   95
said.

LADY WISHFORT

A villain. Superannuated!

FOIBLE

Humh (says he), I hear you are laying designs against me
too (says he), and Mrs. Millamant is to marry my uncle;
(he does not suspect a word of your ladyship); but (says he),   100
I'll fit you for that I warrant you (says he), I'll hamper you
for that (says he)—you and your old frippery too (says he),
I'll handle you!

LADY WISHFORT

Audacious villain! Handle me! Would he durst! Frippery!
Old frippery! Was there ever such a foul-mouthed fellow?   105
I'll be married tomorrow, I'll be contracted tonight!

FOIBLE

The sooner the better madam.

84 *catering* procuring   90 *drawer* tavern-waiter, tapster
92 *Locket's* a famous eating house and tavern in Charing Cross
101 *fit* punish
102 *frippery* old ragged clothes

LADY WISHFORT
  Will Sir Rowland be here, sayest thou? When, Foible?
FOIBLE
  Incontinently madam. No new sheriff's wife expects the
  return of her husband after knighthood with that impatience,   110
  in which Sir Rowland burns for the dear hour of kissing your
  ladyship's hands after dinner.
LADY WISHFORT
  Frippery! Superannuated frippery! I'll frippery the villain:
  I'll reduce him to frippery and rags! A tatterdemalion—I
  hope to see him hung with tatters, like a Long Lane pent-   115
  house, or a gibbet thief! A slander-mouthed railer! I warrant
  the spendthrift prodigal's in debt as much as the million lottery, or the whole court upon a birthday. I'll spoil his credit
  with his tailor! Yes, he shall have my niece with her fortune,
  he shall.   120
FOIBLE
  He! I hope to see him lodge in Ludgate first, and angle into
  Blackfriars for brass farthings with an old mitten!
LADY WISHFORT
  Ay dear Foible; thank thee for that, dear Foible. He has put
  me out of all patience. I shall never recompose my features
  to receive Sir Rowland with any economy of face. This   125
  wretch has fretted me that I am absolutely decayed—look,
  Foible.

112 *hands* Q1 (hand Q2, Ww)

---

109 *Incontinently* immediately
114 *tatterdemalion* ragged beggar
115–16 *Long Lane penthouse.* Long Lane ran from West Smithfield to the
  Barbican and was noted for its impudent rag-sellers. Their stalls may
  have been set up against the houses, with makeshift roofing, or the
  projecting upper stories of the wood-framed buildings may have
  provided their shelter; 'penthouse' can mean either projecting eaves or a
  makeshift shelter set up against a building.
117–18 *million lottery* the government lottery of 1694 (Davis)
118 *court . . . birthday.* The King's birthday was the occasion for wearing
  new clothes.
121 *Ludgate.* Ludgate Prison in Blackfriars held debtors, and the wretched-
  ness of their condition was notorious.
121–2 *angle . . . mitten.* The prisoners would 'fish' for alms with a mitten
  let down on a line from upper windows to passers-by in the street. Brass
  farthings were the smallest units of money.
125 *economy* orderly arrangement

FOIBLE

Your ladyship has frowned a little too rashly indeed, madam.
There are some cracks discernible in the white varnish.

LADY WISHFORT

Let me see the glass. Cracks, sayest thou? Why, I am arrantly   130
flayed! I look like an old peeled wall! Thou must repair me
Foible, before Sir Rowland comes, or I shall never keep up
to my picture.

FOIBLE

I warrant you, madam. A little art once made your picture
like you; and now a little of the same art must make you like   135
your picture. Your picture must sit for you madam.

LADY WISHFORT

But art thou sure Sir Rowland will not fail to come? Or will a
not fail when he does come? Will he be importunate, Foible,
and push? For if he should not be importunate—I shall never
break decorums—I shall die with confusion if I am forced   140
to advance—oh no, I can never advance —I shall swoon if he
should expect advances—no, I hope Sir Rowland is better
bred, than to put a lady to the necessity of breaking her
forms. I won't be too coy neither—I won't give him despair
—but a little disdain is not amiss—a little scorn is alluring.   145

FOIBLE

A little scorn becomes your ladyship.

LADY WISHFORT

Yes, but tenderness becomes me best—a sort of a dyingness
—you see that picture has a sort of a—ha, Foible? A swimminess in the eyes—yes, I'll look so—my niece affects it; but
she wants features. Is Sir Rowland handsome? Let my toilet   150
be removed; I'll dress above. I'll receive Sir Rowland here.
Is he handsome? Don't answer me. I won't know. I'll be
surprised. I'll be taken by surprise.

137–8 *will a not* Q1, Q2, W1 (will he not W2)
148–9 *swimminess* Q1 (swimmingness Q2, Ww)

---

131 *like an old peeled wall* reminiscent of Jonson, *Volpone*, I, v, 58–62:
MOSCA
. . . and those same hanging cheeks,
Couer'd with hide, in stead of skin: (nay, helpe, sir)
That looke like frozen dish-clouts, set on end.
CORVINO
Or, like an old smok'd wall, on which the raine
Ran downe in streakes.

FOIBLE

By storm, madam. Sir Rowland's a brisk man.

LADY WISHFORT

Is he! Oh then he'll importune, if he's a brisk man. I shall   155
save decorums if Sir Rowland importunes. I have a mortal
terror at the apprehension of offending against decorums.
Nothing but importunity can surmount decorums. Oh I'm
glad he's a brisk man. Let my things be removed, good
Foible.   *Exit*   160

Enter MRS. FAINALL

MRS. FAINALL

Oh Foible, I have been in a fright lest I should come too late.
That devil Marwood saw you in the park with Mirabell, and
I'm afraid will discover it to my lady.

FOIBLE

Discover what, madam?

MRS. FAINALL

Nay, nay, put not on that strange face. I am privy to the   165
whole design, and know that Waitwell, to whom thou wert
this morning married, is to personate Mirabell's uncle, and as
such winning my lady, to involve her in those difficulties
from which Mirabell only must release her, by his making
his conditions to have my cousin and her fortune left to her   170
own disposal.

FOIBLE

Oh dear madam, I beg your pardon. It was not my confidence in your ladyship that was deficient; but I thought the
former good correspondence between your ladyship and Mr.
Mirabell might have hindered his communicating this   175
secret.

MRS. FAINALL

Dear Foible, forget that.

FOIBLE

Oh dear madam, Mr. Mirabell is such a sweet winning
gentleman, but your ladyship is the pattern of generosity.
Sweet lady, to be so good! Mr. Mirabell cannot choose but be   180
grateful. I find your ladyship has his heart still. Now madam
I can safely tell your ladyship our success. Mrs. Marwood
had told my lady; but I warrant I managed myself. I turned
it all for the better. I told my lady that Mr. Mirabell railed

158 *Nothing . . . decorums* omitted in Q2, Ww

154 *brisk* sprightly and licentious

at her. I laid horrid things to his charge, I'll vow; and my   185
lady is so incensed, that she'll be contracted to Sir Rowland
tonight, she says. I warrant I worked her up, that he may
have her for asking for, as they say of a Welsh maidenhead.

MRS. FAINALL

Oh rare Foible!

FOIBLE

Madam, I beg your ladyship to acquaint Mr. Mirabell of his   190
success. I would be seen as little as possible to speak to him—
besides, I believe Madam Marwood watches me. She has a
month's mind, but I know Mr. Mirabell can't abide her.

Enter FOOTMAN

John, remove my lady's toilet. Madam, your servant; my
lady is so impatient, I fear she'll come for me if I stay.   195

MRS. FAINALL

I'll go with you up the back stairs lest I should meet her.

Exeunt

Enter MRS. MARWOOD

MRS. MARWOOD

Indeed, Mrs. Engine, is it thus with you? Are you become a
go-between of this importance? Yes, I shall watch you. Why,
this wench is the *passe-partout*, a very master-key to everybody's strongbox. My friend Fainall, have you carried it so   200
swimmingly? I thought there was something in it; but it
seems it's over with you. Your loathing is not from a want
of appetite then, but from a surfeit, else you could never be
so cool to fall from a principal to be an assistant: to procure
for him! A pattern of generosity, that I confess. Well, Mr.   205
Fainall, you have met with your match. Oh man, man!
Woman, woman! The devil's an ass. If I were a painter, I
would draw him like an idiot, a driveller, with a bib and
bells. Man should have his head and horns, and woman the
rest of him. Poor simple fiend! Madam Marwood has a   210
month's mind, but he can't abide her! 'Twere better for him
you had not been his confessor in that affair, without you
could have kept his counsel closer. I shall not prove another
pattern of generosity, and stalk for him till he takes his stand
to aim at a fortune. He has not obliged me to that, with   215

214–15 *and stalk . . . fortune* (omitted Ww)

192–3 *a month's mind* a strong inclination
197 *Mrs. Engine* Mrs Trickery
209 *bells* an attribute of folly

those excesses of himself, and now I'll have none of him. Here comes the good lady, panting ripe, with a heart full of hope and a head full of care, like any chemist upon the day of projection.

Enter LADY WISHFORT

LADY WISHFORT

Oh dear Marwood, what shall I say for this rude forgetful- 220
ness? But my dear friend is all goodness.

MRS. MARWOOD

No apologies, dear madam. I have been very well entertained.

LADY WISHFORT

As I'm a person I am in a very chaos to think I should so
forget myself—but I have such an *olio* of affairs really I know 225
not what to do. (*calls*) Foible! I expect my nephew Sir
Wilfull every moment too—why Foible?—he means to travel
for improvement.

MRS. MARWOOD

Methinks Sir Wilfull should rather think of marrying than
travelling at his years. I hear he is turned of forty. 230

LADY WISHFORT

Oh he's in less danger of being spoiled by his travels; I am
against my nephews marrying too young. It will be time
enough, when he comes back and has acquired discretion to
choose for himself.

MRS. MARWOOD

Methinks Mrs. Millamant and he would make a very fit 235
match. He may travel afterwards. 'Tis a thing very usual
with young gentlemen.

LADY WISHFORT

I promise you I have thought on't; and since 'tis your
judgement, I'll think on't again. I assure you I will; I value
your judgement extremely. On my word, I'll propose it. 240

Enter FOIBLE

Come, come, Foible. I had forgot my nephew will be here
before dinner, I must make haste.

FOIBLE

Mr. Witwoud and Mr. Petulant are come to dine with your
ladyship.

219 *projection* the alchemist's final process for turning base metal into gold
225 *olio* a Spanish or Portuguese stew with a great variety of ingredients

LADY WISHFORT

Oh dear, I can't appear till I'm dressed. Dear Marwood,   245
shall I be free with you again, and beg you to entertain 'em?
I'll make all imaginable haste; dear friend excuse me.

Exeunt LADY WISHFORT *and* FOIBLE

Enter MRS. MILLAMANT *and* MINCING

MILLAMANT

Sure never anything was so inbred as that odious man. Marwood, your servant.

MRS. MARWOOD

You have a colour. What's the matter?   250

MILLAMANT

That horrid fellow Petulant has provoked me into a flame—
I have broke my fan! Mincing, lend me yours. Is not all the
powder out of my hair?

MRS. MARWOOD

No; what has he done?

MILLAMANT

Nay, he has done nothing; he has only talked; nay, he has   255
said nothing neither; but he has contradicted everything that
has been said. For my part, I thought Witwoud and he would
have quarrelled.

MINCING

I vow mem, I thought once they would have fit

MILLAMANT

Well, 'tis a lamentable thing I'll swear, that one has not the   260
liberty of choosing one's acquaintance as one does one's
clothes.

MRS. MARWOOD

If we had the liberty, we should be as weary of one set of
acquaintance, though never so good, as we are of one suit,
though never so fine. A fool and a doily stuff would now   265
and then find days of grace, and be worn for variety.

MILLAMANT

I could consent to wear 'em, if they would wear alike; but
fools never wear out—they are such *drap-de-Berry* things,

---

260 *I'll swear* Q1 (I swear Q2, Ww)
263 *the liberty.* Q1, Q2 (that liberty Ww)

---

259 *fit* Mincing's affected pronunciation for 'fought'
265 *doily* light woollen material for summer use
268 *drap-de-Berry* woollen cloth from Berry in France; of a coarse kind

without one could give 'em to one's chambermaid after a day
or two!   270

MRS. MARWOOD

'Twere better so indeed. Or what think you of the playhouse?
A fine gay glossy fool should be given there, like a new
masking habit, after the masquerade is over and we have
done with the disguise; for a fool's visit is always a disguise,
and never admitted by a woman of wit but to blind her   275
affair with a lover of sense. If you would but appear bare-
faced now, and own Mirabell, you might as easily put off
Petulant and Witwoud as your hood and scarf; and indeed
'tis time, for the town has found it; the secret is grown too
big for the pretence. 'Tis like Mrs. Primly's great belly; she   280
may lace it down before, but it burnishes on her hips. Indeed,
Millamant, you can no more conceal it than my Lady
Strammel can her face, that goodly face, which in defiance of
her Rhenish wine tea will not be comprehended in a mask.

MILLAMANT

I'll take my death, Marwood, you are more censorious than a   285
decayed beauty or a discarded toast. Mincing, tell the men
they may come up. My aunt is not dressing. Their folly is less
provoking than your malice.

Exit MINCING

The town has found it! What has it found? That Mirabell
loves me is no more a secret, than it is a secret that you dis-   290
covered it to my aunt, or than the reason why you discovered
it is a secret.

MRS. MARWOOD

You are nettled.

MILLAMANT

You're mistaken. Ridiculous!

---

287 *dressing* Q1, Q2 (dressing here Ww)

---

273 *habit* costume
280 *Primly*. 'Prim' means affectedly strict, precise, or demure.
281 *burnish* grow plump
283 *Strammel* a lean, gaunt ill-favoured person or animal (OED)
284 *Rhenish wine tea*. Rhine wine was regarded as helpful in reducing
corpulence and high colour (Summers, OED): but Davis thinks thin,
hock-coloured tea may be meant.
286 *discarded toast* person fallen from popularity, whose health is no longer
drunk

MRS. MARWOOD

Indeed my dear you'll tear another fan if you don't mitigate   295
those violent airs.

MILLAMANT

Oh silly! Ha, ha, ha! I could laugh immoderately. Poor
Mirabell! His constancy to me has quite destroyed his
complaisance for all the world beside. I swear I never
enjoined it him to be so coy. If I had the vanity to think   300
he would obey me, I would command him to show more
gallantry; 'tis hardly well-bred to be so particular on one
hand, and so insensible on the other. But I despair to prevail,
and so let him follow his own way. Ha, ha, ha! Pardon me,
dear creature, I must laugh, ha, ha, ha! Though I grant you   305
'tis a little barbarous, ha, ha, ha!

MRS. MARWOOD

What pity 'tis, so much fine raillery, and delivered with so
significant gesture, should be so unhappily directed to mis-
carry.

MILLAMANT

Ha? Dear creature, I ask your pardon; I swear I did not mind   310
you.

MRS. MARWOOD

Mr. Mirabell and you both may think it a thing impossible,
when I shall tell him, by telling you—

MILLAMANT

Oh dear, what? For it is the same thing, if I hear it—ha, ha,
ha!   315

MRS. MARWOOD

That I detest him, hate him, madam.

MILLAMANT

Oh madam, why so do I—and yet the creature loves me, ha,
ha, ha! How can one forbear laughing to think of it? I am a
sybil if I am not amazed to think what he can see in me.
I'll take my death, I think you are handsomer—and within   320
a year or two as young. If you could but stay for me, I should
overtake you—but that cannot be. Well, that thought makes
me melancholy—now I'll be sad.

MRS. MARWOOD

Your merry note may be changed sooner than you think.

310 *Ha* ed. (Hae Q1, Q2, Ww)
323 *melancholy* Q1, Q2 (melancholic Ww)

319 *sybil* prophetess

MILLAMANT

D'ye say so. Then I'm resolved I'll have a song to keep up my   325
spirits.

Enter MINCING

MINCING

The gentlemen stay but to comb, madam, and will wait on
you.

MILLAMANT

Desire Mrs. —— that is in the next room to sing the song I
would have learned yesterday. You shall hear it madam, not   330
that there's any great matter in it, but 'tis agreeable to my
humour.

SONG

Set by Mr. John Eccles, and sung by Mrs. Hodgson

I

Love's but the frailty of the mind
When 'tis not with ambition joined;
A sickly flame, which if not fed, expires;   335
And feeding, wastes in self-consuming fires.

II

'Tis not to wound a wanton boy
Or amorous youth, that gives the joy;
But 'tis the glory to have pierced a swain
For whom inferior beauties sighed in vain.   340

III

Then I alone the conquest prize
When I insult a rival's eyes:
If there's delight in love, 'tis when I see
That heart which others bleed for, bleed for me.

Enter PETULANT *and* WITWOUD

MILLAMANT

Is your animosity composed, gentlemen?   345

332 *and sung . . . Hodgson* Q1, Q2 (omitted Ww)

---

327 *comb.* Combing wigs was a customary masculine mode of conspicuous
leisure.

332 *Mrs. Hodgson.* She had a high reputation as a singer and sang the part of
Juno in *The Judgement of Paris*, for which Congreve much admired her.

WITWOUD

Raillery, raillery, madam, we have no animosity. We hit off a
little wit now and then, but no animosity; the falling out of
wits is like the falling out of lovers—we agree in the main
like treble and bass. Ha, Petulant?

PETULANT

Ay, in the main, but when I have a humour to contradict.　350

WITWOUD

Ay, when he has a humour to contradict, then I contradict
too. What, I know my cue. Then we contradict one another
like two battledores: for contradictions beget one another
like Jews.

PETULANT

If he says black's black—if I have a humour to say 'tis blue—　355
let that pass; all's one for that. If I have a humour to prove it,
it must be granted.

WITWOUD

Not positively must—but it may—it may.

PETULANT

Yes it positive'y must, upon proof positive.

WITWOUD

Ay, upon proof positive it must; but upon proof presump-　360
tive it only may. That's a logical distinction now, madam.

MRS. MARWOOD

I perceive your debates are of importance and very learnedly
handled.

PETULANT

Importance is one thing, and learning's another; but a
debate's a debate, that I assert.　365

WITWOUD

Petulant's an enemy to learning; he relies altogether on his
parts.

PETULANT

No, I'm no enemy to learning; it hurts not me.

MRS. MARWOOD

That's a sign indeed it's no enemy to you.

PETULANT

No, no, it's no enemy to anybody but them that have it.　370

MILLAMANT

Well, an illiterate man's my aversion. I wonder at the impudence of any illiterate man, to offer to make love.

---

353 *battledores* players striking a shuttlecock to and from each other, as in
　badminton

4　*　*

WITWOUD
That I confess I wonder at too.

MILLAMANT
Ah! To marry an ignorant, that can hardly read or write!

PETULANT
Why should a man be ever the further from being married   375
though he can't read, any more than he is from being hanged?
The Ordinary's paid for setting the psalm, and the parish
priest for reading the ceremony; and for the rest which is to
follow in both cases, a man may do it without book—so all's
one for that.   380

MILLAMANT
D'ye hear the creature? Lord, here's company—I'll be gone.
                    Exeunt MILLAMANT *and* MINCING

WITWOUD
In the name of Bartlemew and his fair, what have we here?

MRS. MARWOOD
'Tis your brother, I fancy. Don't you know him?

WITWOUD
Not I—yes, I think it is he; I've almost forgot him; I have
not seen him since the Revolution.   385

Enter SIR WILFULL WITWOUD *in a country riding habit, and* [a]
                    SERVANT *to Lady Wishfort*

SERVANT
Sir, my lady's dressing. Here's company, if you please to
walk in in the mean time.

SIR WILFULL
Dressing! What, it's but morning here, I warrant, with you
in London. We should count it towards afternoon in our
parts, down in Shropshire. Why then belike my aunt han't   390
dined yet—ha, friend?

SERVANT
Your aunt, sir?

---

376 *any more than* Q1, Q2 (than Ww)

377 *Ordinary* the Newgate chaplain
382 *Bartlemew* the fair held on St Bartholomew's Day, 24 August, at
    Smithfield. Jonson's comedy of the same name exhibits some of the
    customary strange sights and alludes to others, such as the bull with
    five legs and two pizzles, which may be in Witwoud's mind as he gazes
    at Sir Wilfull.
385 *the Revolution* that of 1688 which brought William and Mary to the
    throne

SIR WILFULL

My aunt sir, yes my aunt sir, and your lady sir; your lady is
my aunt sir! Why, what, dost thou not know me, friend?
Why then send somebody here that does. How long hast thou   395
lived with thy lady, fellow, ha?

SERVANT

A week sir: longer than anybody in the house except my
lady's woman.

SIR WILFULL

Why then belike thou dost not know thy lady if thou seest
her—ha, friend?   400

SERVANT

Why truly sir, I cannot safely swear to her face in a morning
before she is dressed. 'Tis like I may give a shrewd guess at
her by this time.

SIR WILFULL

Well, prithee try what thou canst do; if thou canst not guess,
enquire her out, dost hear, fellow, and tell her her nephew,   405
Sir Wilfull Witwoud, is in the house.

SERVANT

I shall sir.

SIR WILFULL

Hold ye—hear me friend, a word with you in your ear;
prithee, who are these gallants?

SERVANT

Really sir, I can't tell; here come so many here, 'tis hard to   410
know 'em all.   *Exit*

SIR WILFULL

Oons, this fellow knows less than a starling; I don't think a'
knows his own name.

MRS. MARWOOD

Mr. Witwoud, your brother is not behindhand in forget-
fulness—I fancy he has forgot you, too.   415

WITWOUD

I hope so. The devil take him that remembers first, I say.

SIR WILFULL

Save you, gentlemen and lady.

MRS. MARWOOD

For shame Mr. Witwoud; why won't you speak to him? And
you, sir?

395 *somebody here* Q1, Q2 (somebody hither Ww)
397 *anybody* Q1, Q2, W1 (any W2)

---

412 *Oons* corruption of the oath 'by God's wounds'

WITWOUD

Petulant, speak.   420

PETULANT

And you sir.

SIR WILFULL

No offence, I hope. (*salutes* MRS. MARWOOD)

MRS. MARWOOD

No, sure sir.

WITWOUD

This is a vile dog, I see that already. No offence! Ha, ha, ha,
to him, to him, Petulant! Smoke him!   425

PETULANT

It seems as if you had come a journey, sir—hem, hem.
(*surveying him round*)

SIR WILFULL

Very likely, sir, that it may seem so.

PETULANT

No offence, I hope, sir.

WITWOUD

Smoke the boots, the boots! Petulant, the boots! Ha, ha, ha!

SIR WILFULL

Maybe not sir; thereafter, as 'tis meant, sir.   430

PETULANT

I presume upon the information of your boots.

SIR WILFULL

Why 'tis like you may sir. If you are not satisfied with the
information of my boots, sir, if you will step to the stable you
may enquire further of my horse, sir!

PETULANT

Your horse, sir! Your horse is an ass, sir!   435

SIR WILFULL

Do you speak by way of offence, sir?

MRS. MARWOOD

The gentleman's merry, that's all sir—[*Aside*] 'slife, we shall
have a quarrel betwixt an horse and an ass before they find
one another out—you must not take anything amiss from your
friends, sir. You are among your friends here, though it may   440
be you don't know it. If I am not mistaken, you are Sir
Wilfull Witwoud.

SIR WILFULL

Right, lady; I am Sir Wilfull Witwoud, so I write myself; no

422 *No offence* possibly reminiscent of Falstaff's attempts to excuse his
    insults to Hal (2 *Henry IV*, II, iv, 302, 5, 7) 'No abuse, Hal, o'mine honour,
429 *Smoke* mock

offence to anybody, I hope; and nephew to the Lady
Wishfort of this mansion.   445

MRS. MARWOOD

Don't you know this gentleman, sir?

SIR WILFULL

Hum! What, sure 'tis not—yea, by'r Lady, but 'tis—'sheart I
know not whether 'tis or no—yea but 'tis, by the Wrekin!
Brother Anthony! What Tony i'faith! What, dost thou not
know me? By'r Lady nor I thee, thou art so becravated and   450
beperiwigged! 'Sheart, why dost not speak? Art thou
o'erjoyed?

WITWOUD

Odso brother, is it you? Your servant, brother.

SIR WILFULL

Your servant! Why, yours sir. Your servant again—'sheart,
and your friend and servant to that—and a—(*puff*) and a   455
flapdragon for your service, sir! And a hare's foot, and a
hare's scut for your service sir, an you be so cold and so
courtly!

WITWOUD

No offence I hope, brother.

SIR WILFULL

'Sheart sir, but there is, and much offence! A pox, is this   460
your Inns o' Court breeding, not to know your friends and
your relations, your elders and your betters?

WITWOUD

Why brother Wilfull of Salop, you may be as short as a
Shrewsbury cake if you please, but I tell you 'tis not modish
to know relations in town. You think you're in the country,   465
where great lubberly brothers slabber and kiss one another
when they meet like a call of serjeants. 'Tis not the fashion
here, 'tis not indeed, dear brother.

SIR WILFULL

The fashion's a fool, and you're a fop, dear brother. 'Sheart,

449 *Anthony* Q1, Q2 (Antony Ww)

---

448 *Wrekin* the prominent hill in Shropshire, a famous landmark
456 *flapdragon* a raisin which the players must snatch from burning brandy
    and extinguish by swallowing, in the game of the same name; clap or
    pox (Davis, citing *A Dictionary of the Canting Crew*)
457 *scut* tail
464 *Shrewsbury cake* a kind of shortcake, flat, round, crisp, made in Shrews-
    bury
467 *call of serjeants* a group of barristers who were all called to the bar (i.e.
    admitted to the profession) at the same time

I've suspected this. By'r Lady I conjectured you were a fop   470
since you began to change the style of your letters, and
write in a scrap of paper gilt round the edges, no broader
than a *subpoena*. I might expect this, when you left off
'Honoured Brother,' and 'hoping you are in good health',
and so forth, to begin with a 'Rat me, knight, I'm so sick of a   475
last night's debauch'; 'ods heart, and then tell a familiar tale
of a cock and a bull, and a whore and a bottle, and so
conclude. You could write news before you were out of your
time, when you lived with honest Pumplenose the attorney of
Furnival's Inn: you could entreat to be remembered then to   480
your friends round the Wrekin. We could have gazettes then,
and *Dawks's Letter*, and the weekly bill, till of late days.

PETULANT

'Slife, Witwoud, were you ever an attorney's clerk? Of the
family of the Furnivals? Ha, ha, ha!

WITWOUD

Ay, ay, but that was for a while. Not long, not long; pshaw,   485
I was not in my own power then; an orphan, and this fellow
was my guardian; ay, ay, I was glad to consent to that man to
come to London. He had the disposal of me then. If I had
not agreed to that, I might have been bound prentice to a
felt-maker in Shrewsbury; this fellow would have bound me   490
to a maker of felts!

SIR WILFULL

'Sheart, and better than to be bound to a maker of fops;
where, I suppose, you have served your time, and now you
may set up for yourself.

MRS. MARWOOD

You intend to travel, sir, as I'm informed.   495

SIR WILFULL

Belike I may, madam. I may chance to sail upon the salt
seas, if my mind hold.

PETULANT

And the wind serve.

473 *subpoena* writ issued by Chancery commanding the presence of a de-
    fendant to answer the charge against him
475 *Rat me* corrupt form of the oath 'may God rot me'
479 *Pumplenose* i.e. pimplenose
480 *Furnival's Inn* a subordinate inn of court attached to Lincoln's Inn
481 *gazette* news sheet
482 *Dawks's Letter* a weekly news letter published in Great Carter Lane, St
    Paul's (Summers)
482 *weekly bill* recording deaths in the City of London

SIR WILFULL.

Serve or not serve, I shan't ask licence of you, sir, nor the
weathercock your companion. I direct my discourse to the 500
lady, sir. 'Tis like my aunt may have told you, madam; yes, I
have settled my concerns, I may say now, and am minded to
see foreign parts, if and how the peace holds, whereby, that is,
taxes abate.

MRS. MARWOOD

I thought you had designed for France at all adventures. 505

SIR WILFULL

I can't tell that; 'tis like I may, and 'tis like I may not; I
am somewhat dainty in making a resolution, because when
I make it, I keep it. I don't stand shill I, shall I, then;
if I say't, I'll do't. But I have thoughts to tarry a small matter
in town, to learn somewhat of your lingo first, before I cross 510
the seas. I'd gladly have a spice of your French, as they say,
whereby to hold discourse in foreign countries.

MRS. MARWOOD

Here is an academy in town for that use.

SIR WILFULL

There is? 'Tis like there may.

MRS. MARWOOD

No doubt you will return very much improved. 515

WITWOUD

Yes, refined, like a Dutch skipper from a whale-fishing.

Enter LADY WISHFORT *and* FAINALL

LADY WISHFORT

Nephew, you are welcome.

SIR WILFULL

Aunt, your servant.

FAINALL

Sir Wilfull, your most faithful servant.

SIR WILFULL

Cousin Fainall, give me your hand. 520

LADY WISHFORT

Cousin Witwoud, your servant; Mr. Petulant, your servant;
nephew, you are welcome again. Will you drink anything
after your journey, nephew, before you eat? Dinner's almost
ready.

503 *peace* the Peace of Ryswick (1697) which halted the war with France; it
was broken in 1701.
508 *shill I, shall I* shilly shally, undecided
516 *Dutch skipper.* The Dutch were proverbial for grossness.

SIR WILFULL

I'm very well I thank you, aunt; however, I thank you for 525
your courteous offer. 'Sheart, I was afraid you would have
been in the fashion too, and have remembered to have
forgot your relations. Here's your cousin Tony, belike I
mayn't call him brother for fear of offence.

LADY WISHFORT

Oh he's a rallier, nephew—my cousin's a wit, and your great 530
wits always rally their best friends to choose. When you have
been abroad, nephew, you'll understand raillery better.
(FAINALL *and* MRS. MARWOOD *talk apart*)

SIR WILFULL

Why then let him hold his tongue in the mean time, and rail
when that day comes.

Enter MINCING

MINCING

Mem, I come to acquaint your la'ship that dinner is impa- 535
tient.

SIR WILFULL

Impatient? Why then belike it won't stay till I pull off my
boots! Sweetheart, can you help me to a pair of slippers?
My man's with his horses, I warrant.

LADY WISHFORT

Fie, fie, nephew, you would not pull off your boots here? Go 540
down into the hall—dinner shall stay for you—my nephew's
a little unbred, you'll pardon him, madam. Gentlemen, will
you walk? Marwood—

MRS. MARWOOD

I'll follow you, madam—before Sir Wilfull is ready.

[*Exeunt all but* MRS. MARWOOD *and* FAINALL]

FAINALL

Why then Foible's a bawd, an arrant, rank, match-making 545·
bawd, and I, it seems, am a husband, a rank husband; and
my wife a very arrant, rank wife—all in the way of the world.
'Sdeath, to be an anticipated cuckold, a cuckold in embryo!
Sure I was born with budding antlers like a young satyr or a

---

535 *I come* Q1, Q2, W1 (I am come W2)
548 *an anticipated cuckold* Q1, Q2 (a cuckold by anticipation Ww)

---

531 *to choose* by choice, for preference
549 *satyr* having the head and body of a man and the ears, horns, tail, and
legs of a goat

citizen's child! 'Sdeath, to be out-witted, to be out-jilted, 550
out-matrimonied! If I had kept my speed like a stag, 'twere
somewhat; but to crawl after, with my horns, like a snail, and
outstripped by my wife! 'Tis scurvy wedlock!

MRS. MARWOOD

Then shake it off; you have often wished for an opportunity
to part, and now you have it. But first, prevent their plot; 555
the half of Millamant's fortune is too considerable to be
parted with, to a foe—to Mirabell.

FAINALL

Damn him, that had been mine, had you not made that fond
discovery; that had been forfeited, had they been married.
My wife had added lustre to my horns by that increase of 560
fortune; I could have worn 'em tipped with gold, though
my forehead had been furnished like a deputy-lieutenant's
hall.

MRS. MARWOOD

They may prove a cap of maintenance to you still, if you can
away with your wife; and she's no worse than when you had 565
her; I dare swear she had given up her game before she was
married.

FAINALL

Hum, that may be; she might throw up her cards, but I'll be
hanged if she did not put Pam in her pocket.

MRS. MARWOOD

You married her to keep you; and if you can contrive to have 570

552-3 *and outstripped* Q1 (and be outstripped Q2, Ww)
568-9 *she might . . . pocket* (omitted Ww)

---

550 *citizen's child* the joke about merchants, aldermen, and citizens being
cuckolds was traditional; in *The Old Bachelor*, Bellmour remarks he
must dub an alderman cuckold, 'that he may be of equal Dignity with
the rest of his Brethren' (I, i, 159).

562-3 *deputy lieutenant's hall.* As second most prominent man in the county,
the deputy lieutenant would have a grand house and the great hall had
antlers on the walls; compare Jonson, *The Silent Woman*, IV, v, 111-13:
'but then he is so hung with pikes, halberds, peitronells, callivers, and
muskets, that he lookes like a Iustice of peace's hall:'.

564 *cap of maintenance* 'a heraldic term for the kind of cap with two points
like horns behind, borne in the arms of certain families' (Summers);
the passage is reminiscent of the paradoxical witticisms of Touchstone
on cuckoldom in *As You Like It*, III, iii, 42-54. Dr Johnson commented
(on *Much Ado*, I, i, 208) 'Shakespeare had no mercy upon the poor
cuckold, his horn is an inexhaustible subject of merriment'.

569 *Pam.* Jack of Clubs, highest card in the game of loo; Fainall implies
that Mrs Fainall has kept Mirabell as an 'ace' up her sleeve.

her keep you better than you expected, why should you not
keep her longer than you intended?

FAINALL

The means, the means.

MRS. MARWOOD

Discover to my lady your wife's conduct; threaten to part
with her. My lady loves her, and will come to any composi-   575
tion to save her reputation. Take the opportunity of breaking
it, just upon the discovery of this imposture. My lady will be
enraged beyond bounds and sacrifice niece, and fortune, and
all, at that conjuncture. And let me alone to keep her warm; if
she should flag in her part I will not fail to prompt her.   580

FAINALL

Faith, this has an appearance.

MRS. MARWOOD

I'm sorry I hinted to my lady to endeavour a match between
Millamant and Sir Wilfull; that may be an obstacle.

FAINALL

Oh, for that matter leave me to manage him; I'll disable him
for that. He will drink like a Dane; after dinner I'll set his   585
hand in.

MRS. MARWOOD

Well, how do you stand affected towards your lady?

FAINALL

Why faith I'm thinking of it. Let me see. I am married
already, so that's over. My wife has played the jade with me.
Well, that's over too. I never loved her, or if I had, why that   590
would have been over too by this time. Jealous of her I
cannot be, for I am certain; so there's an end of jealousy.
Weary of her I am, and shall be. No, there's no end of that—
no, no, that were too much to hope. Thus far concerning my
repose. Now for my reputation. As to my own, I married   595
not for it, so that's out of the question; and as to my part in
my wife's, why, she had parted with hers before, so bringing
none to me, she can take none from me. 'Tis against all rule
of play that I should lose to one who has not wherewithal to
stake.   600

MRS. MARWOOD

Besides you forget, marriage is honourable.

575–6 *composition* agreement
581 *appearance* i.e. of likely success
585 *Dane* proverbial for drunkenness
585–6 *set his hand in* start him off

FAINALL

Hum! Faith, and that's well thought on; marriage is honourable, as you say; and if so, wherefore should cuckoldom be a
discredit, being derived from so honourable a root?

MRS. MARWOOD

Nay I know not; if the root be honourable, why not the   605
branches?

FAINALL

So, so, why this point's clear. Well, how do we proceed?

MRS. MARWOOD

I will contrive a letter which shall be delivered to my lady
at the time when that rascal who is to act Sir Rowland is with
her. It shall come as from an unknown hand—for the less I   610
appear to know of the truth, the better I can play the incen-
diary. Besides, I would not have Foible provoked if I could
help it, because you know she knows some passages—nay I
expect all will come out—but let the mine be sprung first,
and then I care not if I'm discovered.   615

FAINALL

If the worst come to the worst, I'll turn my wife to grass. I
have already a deed of settlement of the best part of her
estate, which I wheedled out of her; and that you shall
partake at least.

MRS. MARWOOD

I hope you are convinced that I hate Mirabell. Now you'll   620
be no more jealous.

FAINALL

Jealous, no—by this kiss—let husbands be jealous; but let
the lover still believe. Or, if he doubt, let it be only to endear
his pleasure, and prepare the joy that follows, when he proves
his mistress true. But let husbands' doubts convert to endless   625
jealousy, or, if they have belief, let it corrupt to superstition
and blind credulity. I am single, and will herd no more with
'em. True, I wear the badge, but I'll disown the order; and
since I take my leave of 'em, I care not if I leave 'em a
common motto to their common crest: 630

All husbands must or pain, or shame, endure;
The wise too jealous are, fools too secure.

Exeunt

---

616 *turn . . . to grass* (of horses) retire from service
627 *herd.* This metaphor concludes the imagery of horns.

Act IV, Scene i

Scene continues
Enter LADY WISHFORT *and* FOIBLE

LADY WISHFORT

Is Sir Rowland coming, sayest thou, Foible? And are things
in order?

FOIBLE

Yes madam. I have put wax lights in the sconces, and placed
the footmen in a row in the hall in their best liveries, with
the coachman and postilion to fill up the equipage.   5

LADY WISHFORT

Have you pulvilled the coachman and postilion, that they
may not stink of the stable when Sir Rowland comes by?

FOIBLE

Yes madam.

LADY WISHFORT

And are the dancers and the music ready, that he may be
entertained in all points with correspondence to his passion?   10

FOIBLE

All is ready, madam.

LADY WISHFORT

And—well—and how do I look, Foible?

FOIBLE

Most killing well, madam.

LADY WISHFORT

Well, and how shall I receive him? In what figure shall I give
his heart the first impression? There is a great deal in the first   15
impression. Shall I sit? No, I won't sit, I'll walk. Ay, I'll walk
from the door upon his entrance, and then turn full upon
him. No, that will be too sudden. I'll lie, ay, I'll lie down.
I'll receive him in my little dressing-room, there's a couch—
yes, yes, I'll give the first impression on a couch. I won't lie   20
neither, but loll and lean upon one elbow, with one foot a
little dangling off, jogging in a thoughtful way. Yes; and then
as soon as he appears, start, ay, start and be surprised, and
rise to meet him in a pretty disorder. Yes. Oh, nothing is more
alluring than a levee from a couch in some confusion; it shows   25

5 *fill up the equipage* complete the parade of all the staff
6 *pulvilled* sprinkled with perfumed powder
25 *levee* the action of rising from a bed or couch, usually associated with
   royalty; Lady Wishfort pretends to French sophistication and royal
   status.

the foot to advantage and furnishes with blushes and recom-
posing airs beyond comparison. Hark! There's a coach.

FOIBLE

'Tis he, madam.

LADY WISHFORT

Oh dear, has my nephew made his addresses to Millamant?
I ordered him.   30

FOIBLE

Sir Wilfull is set in to drinking, madam, in the parlour.

LADY WISHFORT

Ods my life I'll send him to her. Call her down, Foible, bring
her hither. I'll send him as I go. When they are together, then
come to me Foible, that I may not be too long alone with
Sir Rowland.   *Exit*   35

Enter MRS. MILLAMANT *and* MRS. FAINALL

FOIBLE

Madam, I stayed here to tell your ladyship that Mr. Mirabell
has waited this half hour for an opportunity to talk with you,
though my lady's orders were to leave you and Sir Wilfull
together. Shall I tell Mr. Mirabell that you are at leisure?

MILLAMANT

No. What would the dear man have? I am thoughtful and   40
would amuse myself; bid him come another time.

  There never yet was woman made
  Nor shall, but to be cursed. (*repeating and walking about*)
That's hard.

MRS. FAINALL

You are very fond of Sir John Suckling today, Millamant,   45
and the poets.

MILLAMANT

He? Ay, and filthy verses; so I am.

FOIBLE

Sir Wilfull is coming madam; shall I send Mr. Mirabell away?

MILLAMANT

Ay, if you please Foible, send him away—or send him hither—
just as you will dear Foible. I think I'll see him—shall I?   50
Ay, let the wretch come.   [*Exit* FOIBLE]
  Thyrsis a youth of the inspired train—(*repeating*)

42-3 *There never . . . cursed* the opening of an untitled poem by Sir John
  Suckling
52 *Thyrsis . . . train* the first line of Edmund Waller's *The Story of Phoebus
  and Daphne, Applied*

Dear Fainall, entertain Sir Wilfull; thou hast philosophy to
undergo a fool, thou art married and hast patience. I would
confer with my own thoughts.   55

MRS. FAINALL

I am obliged to you, that you would make me your proxy in
this affair, but I have business of my own.

Enter SIR WILFULL

Oh Sir Wilfull, you are come at the critical instant. There's
your mistress up to the ears in love and contemplation;
pursue your point, now or never.   60

SIR WILFULL

Yes, my aunt would have it so. I would gladly have been
encouraged with a bottle or two, because I'm somewhat
wary at first, before I am acquainted. (*this while* MILLAMANT
walks about repeating to herself) But I hope after a time
I shall break my mind—that is, upon further acquaintance— 65
so, for the present, cousin, I'll take my leave. If so be you'll
be so kind to make my excuse, I'll return to my company.

MRS. FAINALL

Oh fie Sir Wilfull! What, you must not be daunted.

SIR WILFULL

Daunted? No, that's not it, it is not so much for that—for if
so be that I set on't, I'll do't. But only for the present, 'tis 70
sufficient till further acquaintance, that's all. Your servant.

MRS. FAINALL

Nay, I'll swear you shall never lose so favourable an opportunity if I can help it. I'll leave you together and lock the
door.   *Exit*

SIR WILFULL

Nay nay cousin—I have forgot my gloves—what d'ye do?   75
'Sheart! 'A has locked the door indeed, I think! Nay, cousin
Fainall, open the door! Pshaw, what a vixen trick is this?
Nay, now 'a has seen me too! Cousin, I made bold to pass
through as it were—I think this door's enchanted!

MILLAMANT (*repeating*)

   I prithee spare me, gentle boy,   80
   Press me no more for that slight toy.

---

61 *would have* Q1 (will have Q2, Ww)

---

54 *undergo* endure
80 *I prithee* . . . the opening lines of another untitled Suckling poem;
Millamant mocks Sir Wilfull with these ironically apt quotations.

SIR WILFULL
Anan? Cousin your servant.
MILLAMANT
That foolish trifle of a heart—
Sir Wilfull!
SIR WILFULL
Yes—your servant. No offence I hope, cousin.
MILLAMANT (*repeating*)
I swear it will not do its part   85
Though thou dost thine, employ'st thy power and art.
Natural, easy Suckling!
SIR WILFULL
Anan? Suckling? No such suckling neither, cousin, nor
stripling; I thank heaven I'm no minor.
MILLAMANT
Ah rustic! Ruder than Gothic!   90
SIR WILFULL
Well, well, I shall understand your lingo one of these days,
cousin; in the mean while I must answer in plain English.
MILLAMANT
Have you any business with me, Sir Wilfull?
SIR WILFULL
Not at present, cousin. Yes, I made bold to see, to come and
know if that how you were disposed to fetch a walk this   95
evening; if so be that I might not be troublesome, I would
have sought a walk with you.
MILLAMANT
A walk? What then?
SIR WILFULL
Nay nothing—only for the walk's sake, that's all.
MILLAMANT
I nauseate walking, 'tis a country diversion. I loathe the   100
country and everything that relates to it.

---

97 *sought* ed. (fought Q1, Q2)

87 *easy Suckling* a phrase of the Earl of Rochester's
88 *Suckling*. Sir Wilfull supposes Millamant is calling him a young calf or
lamb.
90 *Gothic* barbarian; reminiscent of *As You Like It*, III, iii, 4–6: 'I am
here with thee and thy goats, as the most capricious poet, honest
Ovid, was among the Goths'
97 *sought*. Q has 'fought' which I take to be a misprint for 'sought' as does
Davis; but Lynch prints 'fought' and notes it was a countrified version
of 'fetched'.

SIR WILFULL

Indeed? Hah! Look ye, look ye, you do? Nay, 'tis like you may. Here are choice of pastimes here in town, as plays and the like—that must be confessed indeed—

MILLAMANT

Ah, *l'étourdie*! I hate the town too.   105

SIR WILFULL

Dear heart, that's much—hah!—that you should hate 'em both! Hah! 'Tis like you may; there are some can't relish the town, and others can't away with the country—'tis like you may be one of those, cousin.

MILLAMANT

Ha, ha, ha! Yes, 'tis like I may. You have nothing further to   110
say to me?

SIR WILFULL

Not at present, cousin; 'tis like, when I have an opportunity to be more private, I may break my mind in some measure—I conjecture you partly guess—however that's as time shall try; but spare to speak and spare to speed, as they say.   115

MILLAMANT

If it is of no great importance, Sir Wilfull, you will oblige me to leave me; I have just now a little business.

SIR WILFULL

Enough, enough, cousin, yes, yes, all a case; when you're disposed, when you're disposed. Now's as well as another time, and another time as well as now. All's one for that. Yes,   120
yes, if your concerns call you, there's no haste; it will keep cold, as they say. Cousin, your servant. I think this door's locked.

MILLAMANT

You may go this way sir.

SIR WILFULL

Your servant; then with your leave I'll return to my com-   125
pany.   *Exit*

MILLAMANT

Ay, ay, ha, ha, ha!
   Like Phoebus sung the no less am'rous boy.

Enter MIRABELL

119 *when you're disposed* (omitted W2)

---

105 *l'étourdie* the giddy town
127 *Like Phoebus* . . . the third line of the Waller poem previously quoted

MIRABELL

Like Daphne she, as lovely and as coy.
Do you lock yourself up from me, to make my search more
curious? Or is this pretty artifice contrived, to signify that   130
here the chase must end, and my pursuit be crowned, for you
can fly no further?

MILLAMANT

Vanity! No. I'll fly and be followed to the last moment,
though I am upon the very verge of matrimony; I expect you
should solicit me as much as if I were wavering at the grate   135
of a monastery, with one foot over the threshold. I'll be
solicited to the very last, nay, and afterwards.

MIRABELL

What, after the last?

MILLAMANT

Oh, I should think I was poor and had nothing to bestow if I
were reduced to an inglorious ease, and freed from the   140
agreeable fatigues of solicitation.

MIRABELL

But do not you know that when favours are conferred upon
instant and tedious solicitation that they diminish in their
value, and that both the giver loses the grace and the receiver
lessens his pleasure?   145

MILLAMANT

It may be in things of common application, but never sure in
love. Oh, I hate a lover that can dare to think he draws a
moment's air independent on the bounty of his mistress.
There is not so impudent a thing in nature as the saucy look
of an assured man, confident of success. The pedantic   150
arrogance of a very husband has not so pragmatical an air.
Ah, I'll never marry, unless I am first made sure of my will
and pleasure.

MIRABELL

Would you have 'em both before marriage, or will you be

128 *Like Daphne* . . . Mirabell completes the couplet; compare *The Man of
      Mode* where Harriet completes Dorimant's couplet (*The Man of Mode*,
      V, ii, 92–3, ed. Brett-Smith [Oxford, 1927])

138 *What, after the last?* The proviso scene allows for a wide, lightly satiric
      survey of follies, affectations, and deceptions by partners in a marriage,
      reminiscent of Truewit's long speeches in II, ii, of Jonson's *The
      Silent Woman*, especially his warning 'euery halfe houres pleasure must be
      bought anew: and with the same paine, and charge, you woo'd her at
      first.'

151 *pragmatical* conceited

contented with the first now, and stay for the other till after   155
grace?

MILLAMANT

Ah don't be impertinent. My dear liberty, shall I leave
thee? My faithful solitude, my darling contemplation, must I
bid you then adieu? Ay-h, adieu; my morning thoughts,
agreeable wakings, indolent slumbers, all ye *douceurs*, ye   160
sommeils du matin, adieu? I can't do't, 'tis more than
impossible. Positively, Mirabell, I'll lie a-bed in a morning
as long as I please.

MIRABELL

Then I'll get up in a morning as early as I please.

MILLAMANT

Ah, idle creature, get up when you will—and, d'ye hear, I   165
won't be called names after I'm married; positively, I won't
be called names.

MIRABELL

Names!

MILLAMANT

Ay, as wife, spouse, my dear, joy, jewel, love, sweetheart, and
the rest of that nauseous cant in which men and their wives   170
are so fulsomely familiar. I shall never bear that. Good
Mirabell, don't let us be familiar or fond, nor kiss before
folks like my Lady Fadler and Sir Francis, nor go to Hyde
Park together the first Sunday in a new chariot, to provoke
eyes and whispers, and then never to be seen there together   175
again; as if we were proud of one another the first week, and
ashamed of one another for ever after. Let us never visit
together, nor go to a play together, but let us be very strange
and well-bred; let us be as strange as if we had been married
a great while, and as well-bred as if we were not married at   180
all.

MIRABELL

Have you any more conditions to offer? Hitherto your
demands are pretty reasonable.

175 *never to be* Q1, Q2 (never be Ww)
177 *for ever after* Q1 (ever after Q2, Ww)

---

170 *nauseous.* Like 'filthy', the word is not used with the strong emphasis it
    has today; affected exaggeration of such words ('dreadful', 'terrible',
    'catastrophic') remains a characteristic of modern affected speech, how-
    ever.
173 *Fadler* one who indulges in fondling
179 *strange* reserved

 - conditions

MILLAMANT

Trifles—as, liberty to pay and receive visits to and from
whom I please, to write and receive letters, without inter-   185
rogatories or wry faces on your part; to wear what I please,
and choose conversation with regard only to my own taste;
to have no obligation upon me to converse with wits that I
don't like, because they are your acquaintance, or to be intimate with fools, because they may be your relations. Come to   190
dinner when I please, dine in my dressing-room when I'm
out of humour, without giving a reason. To have my closet
inviolate, to be sole empress of my tea table, which you
must never presume to approach without first asking leave;
and lastly, wherever I am, you shall always knock at the door   195
before you come in. These articles subscribed, if I continue
to endure you a little longer, I may by degrees dwindle into
a wife.

MIRABELL

Your bill of fare is something advanced in this latter account.
Well, have I liberty to offer conditions, that when you are   200
dwindled into a wife, I may not be beyond measure enlarged
into a husband?

MILLAMANT

You have free leave; propose your utmost, speak and spare
not.

MIRABELL

I thank you. *Imprimis* then, I covenant that your acquaint-   205
ance be general; that you admit no sworn confidante or
intimate of your own sex, no she-friend to screen her affairs
under your countenance and tempt you to make trial of a
mutual secrecy; no decoy-duck to wheedle you a fop,
scrambling to the play in a mask, then bring you home in a   210
pretended fright when you think you shall be found out, and
rail at me for missing the play, and disappointing the frolic,
which you had to pick me up and prove my constancy!

MILLAMANT

Detestable *imprimis*! I go to the play in a mask!

MIRABELL

Item, I article that you continue to like your own face as long   215
as I shall, and while it passes current with me, that you

184 *visits* cf. Truewit: 'Then, you must keep what servants shee please;
what company shee will; that friend must not visit you without her
licence;'
205 *Imprimis* in the first place; a term used in legal contracts. What follows
is reminiscent of *The Silent Woman*, II, ii, 99–105.

endeavour not to new-coin it. To which end, together with
all vizards for the day, I prohibit all masks for the night made
of oiled skins and I know not what—hog's bones, hare's gall,
pig-water, and the marrow of a roasted cat. In short, I forbid   220
all commerce with the gentlewoman in what-d'ye-call-it
Court. *Item*, I shut my doors against all bawds with baskets,
and pennyworth's of muslin, china, fans, atlases, etc. *Item*,
when you shall be breeding—

MILLAMANT

Ah! Name it not.   225

MIRABELL

Which may be presumed, with a blessing on our endeavours—

MILLAMANT

Odious endeavours!

MIRABELL

I denounce against all strait-lacing, squeezing, for a shape,
till you mould my boy's head like a sugar-loaf, and   230
instead of a man-child make me the father to a crooked billet.
Lastly, to the dominion of the tea table I submit, but
with proviso that you exceed not in your province, but
restrain yourself to native and simple tea table drinks, as
tea, chocolate and coffee; as, likewise, to genuine and   235
authorised tea table talk, such as mending of fashions, spoiling reputations, railing at absent friends, and so forth; but
that on no account you encroach upon the men's prerogative
and presume to drink healths or toast fellows; for prevention
of which I banish all foreign forces, all auxiliaries to the tea   240
table, as orange brandy, all aniseed, cinnamon, citron and
Barbadoes waters, together with ratafia and the most noble
spirit of clary. But, for cowslip wine, poppy water and all

231 *me the father* Q1, Q2 (me father Ww)

---

219 *hog's bones* reminiscent of *The Silent Woman*, II, ii, 137–9: 'lies in, a
    moneth, of a new face, all oyle, and birdlime; and ʋises in asses milke,
    and is clens'd with a new *fucus*:'
223 *atlases* rich silk-satin from the Orient, flowered with gold or silver (OED)
229 *strait-lacing* tightly-laced corsets
230 *sugar-loaf* moulded hard refined sugar, in a conical mass; also applied
    figuratively to a conical hill and the conical Tudor and Stuart tall hat
231 *billet* small stick
241 *orange brandy* brandy flavoured with orange-peel
242 *Barbadoes waters* brandy flavoured with orange and lemon peel
243 *clary* a drink made from brandy and clary flowers with the addition of
    sugar, cinnamon, and a little dissolved ambergris

dormitives, those I allow. These provisos admitted, in other
things I may prove a tractable and complying husband.   245

MILLAMANT

Oh horrid provisos! Filthy strong waters! I toast fellows,
odious men! I hate your odious provisos!

MIRABELL

Then we're agreed. Shall I kiss your hand upon the contract? And here comes one to be a witness to the sealing of the
deed.   250

Enter MRS. FAINALL

MILLAMANT

Fainall, what shall I do? Shall I have him? I think I must
have him.

MRS. FAINALL

Ay, ay, take him, take him, what should you do?

MILLAMANT

Well then—I'll take my death I'm in a horrid fright—
Fainall, I shall never say it—well—I think—I'll endure you.   255

MRS. FAINALL

Fie, fie, have him, have him, and tell him so in plain terms;
for I am sure you have a mind to him.

MILLAMANT

Are you? I think I have; and the horrid man looks as if he
thought so too. Well, you ridiculous thing you, I'll have you
—I won't be kissed, nor I won't be thanked—here, kiss my   260
hand though—so, hold your tongue now, and don't say a
word.

MRS. FAINALL

Mirabell, there's a necessity for your obedience: you have
neither time to talk nor stay. My mother is coming, and, in
my conscience, if she should see you, would fall into fits and 265
maybe not recover time enough to return to Sir Rowland,
who as Foible tells me is in a fair way to succeed. Therefore,
spare your ecstasies for another occasion and slip down the
back stairs, where Foible waits to consult you.

MILLAMANT

Ay, go, go. In the mean time I suppose you have said   270
something to please me.

261 *and don't* Q1, Q2 (don't Ww)

244 *dormitives* drinks to induce sleep

MIRABELL

I am all obedience.   *Exit*

MRS. FAINALL

Yonder Sir Wilfull's drunk, and so noisy that my mother
has been forced to leave Sir Rowland to appease him; but he
answers her only with singing and drinking. What they have   275
done by this time I know not, but Petulant and he were upon
quarrelling as I came by.

MILLAMANT

Well, if Mirabell should not make a good husband, I am a
lost thing, for I find I love him violently.

MRS. FAINALL

So it seems, when you mind not what's said to you. If you   280
doubt him, you had best take up with Sir Wilfull.

MILLAMANT

How can you name that superannuated lubber? Foh!

Enter WITWOUD *from drinking*

MRS. FAINALL

So, is the fray made up, that you have left 'em?

WITWOUD

Left 'em? I could stay no longer. I have laughed like ten
christenings; I am tipsy with laughing. If I had stayed any   285
longer I should have burst, I must have been let out and
pieced in the sides like an unsized camlet! Yes, yes, the fray is
composed; my lady came in like a *nolle prosequi* and stopped
their proceedings.

MILLAMANT

What was the dispute?   290

WITWOUD

That's the jest, there was no dispute, they could neither of
'em speak for rage, and so fell a-sputtering at one another
like two roasting apples.

Enter PETULANT *drunk*

275 *they have* Q1, Q2 (they may have Ww)
280 *when you* Q1, Q2 (for you Ww)
289 *their proceedings* Q1, Q2 (the proceedings Ww)

---

287 *pieced* enlarged with pieces of inserted material
287 *unsized camlet* unstiffened material, originally rich and Oriental, but
     subsequently a debased shoddy imitation
288 *nolle prosequi* term for ending legal proceedings

Now Petulant, all's over, all's well; Gad, my head begins to
whim it about! Why dost thou not speak? Thou art both as   295
drunk and as mute as a fish.

PETULANT

Look you Mrs. Millamant, if you can love me, dear nymph—
say it—and that's the conclusion; pass on, or pass off—that's
all.

WITWOUD

Thou hast uttered volumes, folios, in less than *decimo sexto*,   300
my dear Lacedemonian, Sirrah Petulant: thou art an epito-
miser of words.

PETULANT

Witwoud, you are an annihilator of sense.

WITWOUD

Thou art a retailer of phrases, and dost deal in remnants of
remnants, like a maker of pincushions. Thou art in truth   305
(metaphorically speaking) a speaker of shorthand.

PETULANT

Thou art (without a figure) just one half of an ass; and
Baldwin yonder, thy half-brother, is the rest. A gemini of
asses split would make just four of you.

WITWOUD

Thou dost bite, my dear mustard seed; kiss me for that.   310

PETULANT

Stand off! I'll kiss no more males; I have kissed your twin
yonder in a humour of reconciliation till he (*hiccup*) rises
upon my stomach like a radish.

MILLAMANT

Eh! Filthy creature! What was the quarrel?

PETULANT

There was no quarrel. There might have been a quarrel.   315

WITWOUD

If there had been words enow between 'em to have expressed

---

295 *whim it about* spin
300 *decimo sexto* a book of very small size in which each sheet is folded into
   sixteen leaves (whereas a folio is composed of sheets folded into two
   leaves)
301 *Lacedemonian.* Spartan brevity is Petulant's gift.
308 *Baldwin* an ass in the beast epic *Reynard the Fox* reprinted in 1694
   (Davis)
308 *gemini* pair of twins
313 *radish* perhaps reminiscent of Sir Toby's difficulties with pickled
   herring in *Twelfth Night*, I, v, 114

provocation they had gone together by the ears like a pair of
castanets.

PETULANT

You were the quarrel.

MILLAMANT

Me!   320

PETULANT

If I have a humour to quarrel, I can make less matters conclude premises. If you are not handsome, what then, if I have
a humour to prove it? If I shall have my reward, say so;
if not, fight for your face the next time yourself—I'll go sleep.

WITWOUD

Do, wrap thyself up like a woodlouse and dream revenge!   325
And hear me, if thou canst learn to write by tomorrow morning, pen me a challenge: I'll carry it for thee.

PETULANT

Carry your mistress's monkey a spider! Go flea dogs, and
read romances! I'll go to bed to my maid.   *Exit*

MRS. FAINALL

He's horridly drunk. How came you all in this pickle?   330

WITWOUD

A plot, a plot, to get rid of the knight; your husband's advice;
but he sneaked off.

Enter LADY [WISHFORT] *and* SIR WILFULL *drunk*

LADY WISHFORT

Out upon't, out upon't, at years of discretion, and comport
yourself at this rantipole rate?

SIR WILFULL

No offence, aunt.   335

LADY WISHFORT

Offence! As I'm a person I'm ashamed of you—fogh! How

---

325 *woodlouse* reminiscent of *The Silent Woman*, II, iv, 140–42: 'Or a
   snaile, or a hog-louse: I would roule my selfe vp for this day, introth,
   they should not vnwinde me.'
328 *Carry . . . spider* bawdy, as in Marston, *The Malcontent* (ed. Bernard
   Harris, 1968) I, iii, 40–41:
      PIETRO
      How dost thou live nowadays, Malevole?
      MALEVOLE
      Why, like the knight, Sir Patrick Penlolians, with killing of spiders
      for my lady's monkey.
334 *rantipole* grossly ill-mannered

you stink of wine! D'ye think my niece will ever endure such
a borachio? You're an absolute borachio!

SIR WILFULL

Borachio!

LADY WISHFORT

At a time when you should commence an amour and put   340
your best foot foremost—

SIR WILFULL

'Sheart, an you grutch me your liquor, make a bill—give me
more drink, and take my purse! (*sings*)

       Prithee fill me the glass
       Till it laugh in my face   345
       With ale that is potent and mellow;
       He that whines for a lass
       Is an ignorant ass,
       For a bumper has not its fellow.

But if you would have me marry my cousin, say the word   350
and I'll do't; Wilfull will do't, that's the word; Wilfull will
do't, that's my crest; my motto I have forgot.

LADY WISHFORT

My nephew's a little overtaken, cousin, but 'tis with drinking
your health; o' my word you are obliged to him.

SIR WILFULL

In vino veritas, aunt. If I drunk your health today, cousin, I   355
am a borachio! But, if you have a mind to be married, say the
word, and send for the piper, Wilfull will do't. If not, dust it
away, and let's have t'other round. Tony! Ods heart where's
Tony? Tony's an honest fellow, but he spits after a bumper,
and that's a fault. (*sings*)   360

       We'll drink and we'll never ha' done boys,
       Put the glass then around with the sun boys,
       Let Apollo's example invite us;
       For he's drunk every night
       And that makes him so bright   365
       That he's able next morning to light us.

---

345 *laugh* Q1, Ww (laughs Q2)

---

338 *borachio* the Spanish leathern bottle for wine, hence the term for drunk-
    ard and the name of the minor character in *Much Ado About Nothing*
342 *grutch* begrudge
349 *bumper* brim-full glass of wine
355 *In vino veritas* drunkards speak the truth

The sun's a good pimple, an honest soaker, he has a cellar
at your Antipodes. If I travel, aunt, I touch at your Antipodes—your Antipodes are a good rascally sort of topsy-
turvy fellows—if I had a bumper I'd stand upon my head   370
and drink a health to 'em. A match or no match, cousin with
the hard name? Aunt, Wilfull will do't: if she has her
maidenhead let her look to't; if she has not, let her keep her
own counsel in the meantime, and cry out at the nine
months' end.   375

MILLAMANT

Your pardon madam, I can stay no longer—Sir Wilfull
grows very powerful—egh! How he smells! I shall be
overcome if I stay. Come, cousin.

Exeunt MILLAMANT *and* MRS. FAINALL

LADY WISHFORT

Smells! He would poison a tallow chandler and his family.
Beastly creature, I know not what to do with him. Travel,   380
quotha! Ay, travel, travel, get thee gone, get thee but far
enough, to the Saracens, or the Tartars, or the Turks, for
thou art not fit to live in a Christian commonwealth, thou
beastly pagan!

SIR WILFULL

Turks? no, no Turks, aunt; your Turks are infidels, and   385

367 *pimple* good companion
368 *Antipodes* perhaps reminiscent of *Much Ado*, II, i, 234–40. Popular
   notions about men who lived upside down on the other side of the
   world derive principally from Mandeville's *Voyages*, a source for the
   play *The Antipodes* by Richard Brome (1638) in which the question is
   posed
                      what people
        Are they of the Antipodes? Are they not such
        As Mandeville writes of, without heads or necks,
        Having their eyes plac'd on their shoulders, and
        Their mouths amidst their breasts? (I, vi, 98–102, ed. A. Haaker,
        1967)

   In this play Peregrine has become mad with reading traveller's tales, and
   is deluded that he is in the Antipodes, where he finds such topsy-turvy
   marvels as aldermen who love poetry and honest lawyers. Sir Wilfull, as
   the embodiment of saturnalian spirit in the play, and a would-be
   traveller, is appropriately associated with Brome's play and his Peregrine.
377 *smells* Millamant finds Sir Wilfull's insinuations as repellent as his smell;
   he smells personally and metaphorically.
379 *tallow chandler* maker of tallow candles; Sir Fopling objects to their
   smell: 'How can you breathe in a Room where there's Grease frying!'
   (*Man of Mode*, IV, i, 283).

believe not in the grape. Your Mahometan, your Mussul-
man, is a dry stinkard—no offence, aunt. My map says that
your Turk is not so honest a man as your Christian; I cannot
find by the map that your Mufti is orthodox; whereby it is a
plain case, that orthodox is a hard word, aunt, and (*hiccup*)   390
Greek for claret. (*sings*)

> To drink is a Christian diversion,
> Unknown to the Turk and the Persian;
> Let Mahometan fools
> Live by heathenish rules   395
> And be damned over tea cups and coffee!
> But let British lads sing,
> Crown a health to the king,
> And a fig for your sultan and sophy!

Ah Tony!   400

Enter FOIBLE, *and whispers* LADY [WISHFORT]

LADY WISHFORT

Sir Rowland impatient? Good lack! What shall I do with
this beastly tumbril? Go lie down and sleep, you sot, or as
I'm a person I'll have you bastinadoed with broomsticks!
Call up the wenches.   *Exit* FOIBLE

SIR WILFULL

Ahey! Wenches! Where are the wenches?   405

LADY WISHFORT

Dear cousin Witwoud, get him away, and you will bind me to
you inviolably. I have an affair of moment that invades me
with some precipitation. You will oblige me to all futurity.

WITWOUD

Come, knight. Pox on him, I don't know what to say to him.
Will you go to a cock-match?   410

---

393 *Turk and* Q1, Q2 (Turk or Ww)
404 *wenches* Q1, Q2 (wenches with broomsticks Ww)

---

387 *dry* teetotal
389 *Mufti*. Mohammedan priest
391 *Greek* Jaques in *As You Like It*, II, v, 54–5 describes 'ducdame'
     as a 'Greek invocation, to call fools into a circle'.
402 *tumbril* heavy cart
403 *bastinadoed* beaten on the soles of the feet, or, simply, punished with a
     beating
410 *cock-match* cock-fight

SIR WILFULL

With a wench, Tony? Is she a shake-bag, sirrah? Let me bite
your cheek for that.

WITWOUD

Horrible! He has a breath like a bagpipe. Ay, ay, come, will
you march, my Salopian?

SIR WILFULL

Lead on little Tony—I'll follow thee my Anthony, my   415
Tantony; sirrah, thou shalt be my Tantony, and I'll be thy
pig—
And a fig for your sultan and sophy.

Exit singing with WITWOUD

LADY WISHFORT

This will never do. It will never make a match—at least
before he has been abroad.   420

Enter WAITWELL *disguised as for Sir Rowland*

Dear Sir Rowland, I am confounded with confusion at the
retrospection of my own rudeness. I have more pardons to
ask than the Pope distributes in the year of Jubilee; but I hope
where there is likely to be so near an alliance, we may unbend
the severity of decorum, and dispense with a little ceremony.   425

WAITWELL

My impatience, madam, is the effect of my transport; and till

411 *shake-bag* game-cock, the largest and strongest kind of fighting-cock and
able to give any opponent a good fight

414 *Salopian.* Shropshire man

416-17 *Tantony . . . pig.* The point of the jest is in the contrast between
Witwoud's thinness and Sir Wilfull's fatness (compare *2 Henry IV*,
I, ii, 12–14 where Falstaff says to his boy 'I do here walk before thee
like a sow that hath overwhelm'd all her litter but one'). There are
contradictory associations in the term Tantony pig, since in religious
art St Anthony has a pig as an attribute to mark his triumph over
gluttony and the devil. The Hospital Brothers of St Anthony of Clermont
had a privileged herd of pigs famous for their fatness; a Tantony pig
could be a very large pig, therefore. On the other hand it could mean the
smallest pig in a litter, proverbial for obsequiousness; if this is the
sense, Sir Wilfull jestingly reverses the obvious application to Witwoud;
but the more likely sense is that of extra fatness.

418 *sophy* the name of the Persian dynasty of Shahs was Sufi

423 *year of Jubilee* a year in which the Pope proclaimed remission of punish-
ments imposed for sin: 1700, the year of the play's first performance,
was a Jubilee Year: but there had been a much talked-of Jubilee in
1691, alluded to in Farquhar's play *The Constant Couple: or, a Trip to
the Jubilee* (1699).

I have the possession of your adorable person, I am tantalized
on a rack, and do but hang, madam, on the tenter of expectation.

LADY WISHFORT

You have excess of gallantry Sir Rowland, and press things   430
to a conclusion with a most prevailing vehemence. But a day
or two for decency of marriage—

WAITWELL

For decency of funeral, madam. The delay will break my
heart—or, if that should fail, I shall be poisoned. My nephew
will get an inkling of my designs and poison me—and I   435
would willingly starve him before I die—I would gladly go
out of the world with that satisfaction. That would be some
comfort to me, if I could but live so long as to be revenged on
that unnatural viper.

LADY WISHFORT

Is he so unnatural, say you? Truly I would contribute much   440
both to the saving of your life and the accomplishment of
your revenge; not that I respect myself, though he has been a
perfidious wretch to me.

WAITWELL

Perfidious to you!

LADY WISHFORT

Oh Sir Rowland, the hours that he has died away at my feet,   445
the tears that he has shed, the oaths that he has sworn, the
palpitations that he has felt, the trances, and the tremblings,
the ardours and the ecstasies, the kneelings and the risings,
the heart-heavings and the hand-grippings, the pangs and
the pathetic regards of his protesting eyes, oh no memory   450
can register!

WAITWELL

What, my rival! Is the rebel my rival? 'A dies!

LADY WISHFORT

No, don't kill him at once Sir Rowland, starve him gradually,
inch by inch.

WAITWELL

I'll do't. In three weeks he shall be barefoot; in a month out   455
at knees with begging an alms. He shall starve upward and

---

428 *a rack* Q1 (the rack Q2, Ww)

---

428 *tenter* associated with suspense or tension. The tenter was a wooden
frame with hooks on which cloth was stretched after milling so that it
would dry without distortion or shrinking.

439 *viper*. In the Aesop fable the viper stung the husbandman who nursed it.

upward, till he has nothing living but his head, and then go
out in a stink, like a candle's end upon a save-all.

LADY WISHFORT

Well, Sir Rowland, you have the way; you are no novice
in the labyrinth of love, you have the clue. But, as I am a   460
person, Sir Rowland, you must not attribute my yielding to
any sinister appetite, or indigestion of widowhood, nor
impute my complacency to any lethargy of continence.
I hope you do not think me prone to any iteration of
nuptials—   465

WAITWELL

Far be it from me—

LADY WISHFORT

If you do, I protest I must recede—or think that I have
made a prostitution of decorums, but in the vehemence of
compassion, and to save the life of a person of so much
importance—   470

WAITWELL

I esteem it so—

LADY WISHFORT

Or else you wrong my condescension—

WAITWELL

I do not, I do not—

LADY WISHFORT

Indeed you do—

WAITWELL

I do not, fair shrine of virtue—   475

LADY WISHFORT

If you think the least scruple of carnality was an ingredi-
ent—

WAITWELL

Dear madam, no. You are all camphire and frankincense, all
chastity and odour—

---

464 *iteration* ed. (interation Q1, Q2)

---

458 *save-all* a small metal dish with a pin projecting from the centre on which
the candle end was fixed so that the candle burned right to the end
462 *sinister appetite.* Lady Wishfort's cumbrous circumlocutions all amount
to the same claim: that sexual desire is not a motive in her agreement to
marry.
478 *camphire.* Camphor was supposed to lessen desire.
478 *frankincense* an aromatic gum resin from the tree *Boswellia*; 'frank'
seems to have originally meant 'valuable' (OED).

LADY WISHFORT
Or that—   480

Enter FOIBLE

FOIBLE
Madam, the dancers are ready, and there's one with a letter
who must deliver it into your own hands.

LADY WISHFORT
Sir Rowland, will you give me leave? Think favourably,
judge candidly, and conclude you have found a person who
would suffer racks in honour's cause, dear Sir Rowland, and   485
will wait on you incessantly.   *Exit*

WAITWELL
Fie, fie, what a slavery have I undergone! Spouse, hast thou
any cordial—I want spirits.

FOIBLE
What a washy rogue art thou, to pant thus for a quarter
of an hour's lying and swearing to a fine lady!   490

WAITWELL
Oh, she is the antidote to desire. Spouse, thou wilt fare the
worse for't. I shall have no appetite to iteration of nuptials
this eight and forty hours! By this hand, I'd rather be a chairman in the dog-days than act Sir Rowland, till this time
tomorrow.   495

Enter LADY WISHFORT *with a letter*

LADY WISHFORT
Call in the dancers. Sir Rowland, we'll sit if you please and
see the entertainment.

Dance

Now with your permission Sir Rowland I will peruse my
letter. I would open it in your presence, because I would not
make you uneasy. If it should make you uneasy I would   500
burn it. Speak if it does—but you may see by the superscription it is like a woman's hand.

FOIBLE [*Aside to* WAITWELL]
By heaven! Mrs. Marwood's, I know it. My heart aches! Get
it from her!

501–2 *by the superscription it is like* Q1, Q2 (the superscription is like
Ww)

---

489 *washy* wishy-washy, weak
493–4 *chairman in the dog-days* sedan-chair bearer in the hottest days of
summer. Two men carried the completely enclosed chair in which the
passenger sat.

WAITWELL

A woman's hand? No madam, that's no woman's hand, I see   505
that already: that's somebody whose throat must be cut.

LADY WISHFORT

Nay Sir Rowland, since you give me a proof of your passion
by your jealousy, I promise you I'll make you a return, by a
frank communication. You shall see it. We'll open it
together. Look you here. (*reads*) 'Madam, though unknown   510
to you'—look you there, 'tis from nobody that I know—'I
have that honour for your character, that I think myself
obliged to let you know you are abused. He who pretends
to be Sir Rowland is a cheat and a rascal'—
Oh heavens! What's this?   515

FOIBLE

Unfortunate. All's ruined.

WAITWELL

How, how? Let me see, let me see! (*reading*) 'A rascal and
disguised and suborned for that imposture'—oh villainy!
Oh villainy!—'by the contrivance of'—

LADY WISHFORT

I shall faint, I shall die, I shall die! Oh!   520

FOIBLE [*Aside to* WAITWELL]

Say 'tis your nephew's hand—quickly, his plot—swear,
swear it!

WAITWELL

Here's a villain! Madam, don't you perceive it, don't you
see it?

LADY WISHFORT

Too well, too well. I have seen too much.   525

WAITWELL

I told you at first I knew the hand. A woman's hand? The
rascal writes a sort of a large hand, your Roman hand. I saw
there was a throat to be cut presently! If he were my son—as
he is my nephew—I'd pistol him!

FOIBLE

Oh treachery! But are you sure, Sir Rowland, it is his   530
writing?

---

520 *I shall die, I shall die! Oh!* Q1 (I shall die! Oh! Q2, Ww)

---

527 *Roman hand* round and bold handwriting; perhaps reminiscent of
Malvolio (*Twelfth Night*, III, iv, 29) insinuating to Olivia that he
recognises her as the author of the letter commending his yellow stock-
ings: 'I think we do know the sweet Roman hand'

WAITWELL

Sure? Am I here? Do I live? Do I lose this pearl of India? I have twenty letters in my pocket from him in the same character.

LADY WISHFORT

How!   535

FOIBLE

Oh what luck it is Sir Rowland that you were present at this juncture! This was the business that brought Mr. Mirabell disguised to Madam Millamant this afternoon. I thought something was contriving when he stole by me and would have hid his face.   540

LADY WISHFORT

How, how! I heard the villain was in the house, indeed, and now I remember, my niece went away abruptly when Sir Wilfull was to have made his addresses.

FOIBLE

Then, then madam, Mr. Mirabell waited for her in her chamber; but I would not tell your ladyship to discompose 545 you when you were to receive Sir Rowland.

WAITWELL

Enough! His date is short.

FOIBLE

No, good Sir Rowland, don't incur the law.

WAITWELL

Law? I care not for law. I can but die, and 'tis in a good cause. My lady shall be satisfied of my truth and innocence, 550 though it cost me my life.

LADY WISHFORT

No, dear Sir Rowland, don't fight, if you should be killed I must never show my face; or hanged—oh consider my reputation, Sir Rowland! No, you shan't fight. I'll go in and examine my niece; I'll make her confess. I conjure you 555 Sir Rowland, by all your love, not to fight.

WAITWELL

I am charmed, madam; I obey. But some proof you must let me give you. I'll go for a black box which contains the writings of my whole estate, and deliver that into your hands.   560

LADY WISHFORT

Ay, dear Sir Rowland, that will be some comfort; bring the black box.

534 *character* style of handwriting
547 *His date is short.* He dies shortly.

5

WAITWELL

And may·I presume to bring a contract to be signed this
night? May I hope so far?

LADY WISHFORT

Bring what you will; but come alive, pray come alive. Oh,   565
this is a happy discovery!

WAITWELL

Dead or alive I'll come, and married we will be in spite of
treachery; ay, and get an heir that shall defeat the last
remaining glimpse of hope in my abandoned nephew.
Come, my buxom widow!   570
    Ere long you shall substantial proof receive
    That I'm an arrant knight—

FOIBLE [*Aside*]   Or arrant knave.   *Exeunt*

Act V, Scene i

Scene continues
Enter LADY WISHFORT *and* FOIBLE

LADY WISHFORT

Out of my house, out of my house, thou viper, thou serpent
that I have fostered! Thou bosom traitress, that I raised from
nothing, begone, begone, begone! Go! Go! That I took
from washing of old gauze and weaving of dead hair, with a
bleak blue nose, over a chafing dish of starved embers, and   5

---

572 *an arrant knight* punning on the phrase 'knight-errant' and 'arrant'
    = 'knavish'
  1 *viper*. The serpent stung the husbandman who nursed it. Lady Wish-
    fort's tirade has close connections with the flyting match between
    Subtle and Face in Jonson, *The Alchemist*, I, i, 25–110; see Subtle's
    taunt

            Thou vermine, hauc I tane thee, out of dung,
            So poore, so wretched, when no liuing thing
            Would keepe thee companie, but a spider, or worse?
            Rais'd thee from broomes, and dust, and watring pots?

  4 *gauze* thin transparent fabric, silk linen or cotton
  4 *weaving of dead hair* making wigs
  5 *bleak blue nose*. Face taunts Subtle with finding him
                        at *pie-corner*,
            Taking your meale of steeme in, from cookes stalls,
            Where, like the father of hunger, you did walke
            Piteously costiue, with your pinch'd-horne-nose (25–8).
  5 *chafing dish* vessel holding burning coal to warm dishes placed on it

dining behind a traverse rag, in a shop no bigger than a
birdcage! Go, go, starve again! Do! Do!

FOIBLE

Dear madam, I'll beg pardon on my knees.

LADY WISHFORT

Away, out, out! Go set up for yourself again! Do, drive a
trade, do! With your threepennyworth of small ware,   10
flaunting upon a packthread, under a brandy-seller's bulk, or
against a dead wall by a ballad-monger! Go hang out an old
frisoneer gorget, with a yard of yellow colberteen again, do!
An old gnawed mask, two rows of pins and a child's fiddle, a
glass necklace with the beads broken, and a quilted nightcap   15
with one ear! Go, go, drive a trade! These were your
commodities, you treacherous trull, this was your merchandise you dealt in, when I took you into my house,
placed you next myself, and made you governante of my whole
family. You have forgot this, have you, now you have   20
feathered your nest?

FOIBLE

No, no, dear madam. Do but hear me, have but a moment's
patience, I'll confess all. Mr. Mirabell seduced me. I am not
the first that he has wheedled with his dissembling tongue.
Your ladyship's own wisdom has been deluded by him; then   25
how should I, a poor ignorant, defend myself? Oh madam,
if you knew but what he promised me, and how he assured
me your ladyship should come to no damage; or else the
wealth of the Indies should not have bribed me to conspire

17–18 *your merchandise* Q1, Q2 (the merchandise Ww)

---

6 *traverse rag* tattered curtain

11 *flaunting upon a packthread.* The phrase 'upon a packthread' could be
analogous to 'on a shoestring' and packthread certainly has associations
of poverty and toughness: carriers, heavy bundles. However, the
phrase most probably means: 'displaying yourself impudently on a
drum of packthread', though the OED records Middleton, *The Black
Book*: 'apparelled in villainous packthread'. Lady Wishfort implies
that Foible would offer more than her small ware for sale.

11 *bulk* stall

12 *dead wall* a continuous wall, with the suggestion of monotony, dreari-
ness, slum areas

12 *ballad-monger* a beggarly occupation

13 *frisoneer gorget* stiff neckpiece (French, *gorge*, throat) made of Fries-
land stuff

13 *colberteen* cheap lace

19 *governante* housekeeper

against so good, so sweet, so kind a lady as you have been   30
to me.

LADY WISHFORT

No damage? What, to betray me, to marry me to a cast
servingman? To make me a receptacle, an hospital for a
decayed pimp? No damage? Oh thou frontless impudence—
more than a big-bellied actress!   35

FOIBLE

Pray do but hear me madam, he could not marry your ladyship, madam, no indeed. His marriage was to have been void
in law, for he was married to me first, to secure your ladyship.
He could not have bedded your ladyship; for if he had con-
summated with your ladyship he must have run the risk of   40
the law and been put upon his clergy. Yes indeed; I enquired
of the law in that case before I would meddle or make.

LADY WISHFORT

What, then I have been your property, have I? I have been
convenient to you, it seems, while you were catering for
Mirabell. I have been broker for you! What, have you made a   45
passive bawd of me? This exceeds all precedent; I am brought
to fine uses, to become a botcher of secondhand marriages
between Abigails and Andrews! I'll couple you, yes, I'll
baste you together, you and your Philander! I'll Duke's
Place you, as I'm a person! Your turtle is in custody   50
already: you shall coo in the same cage, if there be constable
or warrant in the parish!   *Exit*

FOIBLE

Oh that ever I was born, oh that I was ever married! A bride,
ay, I shall be a Bridewell bride! Oh!

Enter MRS. FAINALL

---

51 *constable* Q1, Q2, W1 (a constable W2)

---

34 *frontless* shameless
41 *put upon his clergy.* A criminal who could read and write might claim
'benefit of clergy' to escape the death penalty (Lynch).
42 *meddle or make* co-operate
45 *broker* second-hand dealer, hence procurer, pimp, bawd
48 *Abigails and Andrews* maidservants and manservants
49 *baste* flog
49 *Philander* lover
49–50 *Duke's Place* irregular marriages were notorious at St James's
Church there
54 *Bridewell* the London prison where beating hemp was a punishment for
women prisoners

MRS. FAINALL

Poor Foible, what's the matter?   55

FOIBLE

Oh madam, my lady's gone for a constable; I shall be had to a
justice, and put to Bridewell to beat hemp. Poor Waitwell's
gone to prison already.

MRS. FAINALL

Have a good heart, Foible, Mirabell's gone to give security
for him; this is all Marwood's and my husband's doing.   60

FOIBLE

Yes, yes, I know it madam. She was in my lady's closet, and
overheard all that you said to me before dinner. She sent the
letter to my lady, and that missing effect, Mr. Fainall laid this
plot to arrest Waitwell when he pretended to go for the
papers; and in the mean time Mrs. Marwood declared all   65
to my lady.

MRS. FAINALL

Was there no mention made of me in the letter? My mother
does not suspect my being in the confederacy? I fancy Marwood has not told her, though she has told my husband.

FOIBLE

Yes madam, but my lady did not see that part—we stifled the   70
letter before she read so far. Has that mischievous devil told
Mr. Fainall of your ladyship then?

MRS. FAINALL

Ay, all's out, my affair with Mirabell, everything, discovered. This is the last day of our living together, that's
my comfort.   75

FOIBLE

Indeed madam, and so 'tis a comfort if you knew all. He has
been even with your ladyship; which I could have told you
long enough since, but I love to keep peace and quietness by
my good will; I had rather bring friends together than set
'em at distance. But Mrs. Marwood and he are nearer related   80
than ever their parents thought for.

MRS. FAINALL

Say'st thou so, Foible? Canst thou prove this?

FOIBLE

I can take my oath of it, madam, so can Mrs. Mincing. We
have had many a fair word from Madam Marwood, to conceal something that passed in our chamber one evening when   85
you were at Hyde Park, and we were thought to have gone a-
walking. But we went up unawares, though we were sworn
to secrecy too. Madam Marwood took a book and swore us

upon it; but it was but a book of verses and poems, so as long
as it was not a Bible oath, we may break it with a safe   90
conscience.

MRS. FAINALL

This discovery is the most opportune thing I could wish.
Now Mincing?

Enter MINCING

MINCING

My lady would speak with Mrs. Foible, mem. Mr. Mirabell
is with her; he has set your spouse at liberty, Mrs. Foible,   95
and would have you hide yourself in my lady's closet, till my
old lady's anger is abated. Oh, my old lady is in a perilous
passion at something Mr. Fainall has said; he swears, and my
old lady cries. There's a fearful hurricane, I vow. He says,
mem, how that he'll have my lady's fortune made over to   100
him, or he'll be divorced.

MRS. FAINALL

Does your lady and Mirabell know that?

MINCING

Yes mem, they have sent me to see if Sir Wilfull be sober,
and to bring him to them. My lady is resolved to have him
I think, rather than lose such a vast sum as six thousand   105
pound. Oh come Mrs. Foible, I hear my old lady.

MRS. FAINALL

Foible, you must tell Mincing that she must prepare to vouch
when I call her.

FOIBLE

Yes, yes, madam.

MINCING

Oh yes mem, I'll vouch anything for your ladyship's service,   110
be what it will.   *Exeunt* MINCING *and* FOIBLE

Enter LADY WISHFORT *and* MRS. MARWOOD

LADY WISHFORT

Oh my dear friend, how can I enumerate the benefits that
I have received from your goodness? To you I owe the
timely discovery of the false vows of Mirabell; to you the
detection of the impostor Sir Rowland. And now you are be-   115
come an intercessor with my son-in-law, to save the honour

89 *verses and poems* Q1, Q2 (poems Ww)
89–90 *as long as* Q1 (long as Q2, Ww)
102 *lady and* Q1, Q2 (lady or Ww)
114–15 *to you the detection* Q1, Q2 (to you I owe the detection Ww)

of my house, and compound for the frailties of my daughter.
Well, friend, you are enough to reconcile me to the bad
world, or else I would retire to deserts and solitudes, and
feed harmless sheep by groves and purling streams. Dear   120
Marwood, let us leave the world, and retire by ourselves
and be shepherdesses.

MRS. MARWOOD

Let us first dispatch the affair in hand, madam, we shall have
leisure to think of retirement afterwards. Here is one who is
concerned in the treaty.   125

LADY WISHFORT

Oh daughter, daughter, is it possible thou shouldst be my
child, bone of my bone and flesh of my flesh, and, as I may
say, another me, and yet transgress the most minute particle
of severe virtue? Is it possible you should lean aside to
iniquity, who have been cast in the direct mould of virtue?   130
I have not only been a mould but a pattern for you, and a
model for you, after you were brought into the world.

MRS. FAINALL

I don't understand your ladyship.

LADY WISHFORT

Not understand? Why, have you not been naught? Have you
not been sophisticated? Not understand? Here I am ruined   135
to compound for your caprices and your cuckoldoms;
I must pawn my plate, and my jewels, and ruin my niece, and
all little enough—

MRS. FAINALL

I am wronged and abused, and so are you. 'Tis a false accusation, as false as hell, as false as your friend there, ay or your   140
friend's friend, my false husband.

MRS. MARWOOD

My friend, Mrs. Fainall? Your husband my friend? What do
you mean?

MRS. FAINALL

I know what I mean, madam, and so do you, and so shall
the world at a time convenient.   145

MRS. MARWOOD

I am sorry to see you so passionate, madam. More temper
would look more like innocence; but I have done. I am
sorry my zeal to serve your ladyship should admit of miscon-
struction, or make me liable to affronts. You will pardon me,

117 *compound* settle by making concessions
134 *naught* lewd
135 *sophisticated* corrupted

madam, if I meddle no more with an affair in which I am not   150
personally concerned.

LADY WISHFORT

Oh dear friend, I am so ashamed that you should meet with
such returns;—[*to* MRS. FAINALL] you ought to ask pardon
on your knees, ungrateful creature! She deserves more from
you than all your life can accomplish. [*to* MRS. MARWOOD]   155
Oh, don't leave me destitute in this perplexity! No, stick to
me, my good genius.

MRS. FAINALL

I tell you madam you're abused! Stick to you? Ay, like a
leech, to suck your best blood—she'll drop off when she's
full. Madam, you sha' not pawn a bodkin, nor part with a   160
brass counter, in composition for me! I defy 'em all; let 'em
prove their aspersions, I know my own innocence, and dare
stand by a trial.   *Exit*

LADY WISHFORT

Why, if she should be innocent, if she should be wronged
after all, ha? I don't know what to think—and I promise you,   165
her education has been unexceptionable—I may say it, for I
chiefly made it my own care to initiate her very infancy in the
rudiments of virtue, and to impress upon her tender years a
young odium and aversion to the very sight of men. Ay,
friend, she would ha' shrieked if she had but seen a man, till   170
she was in her teens; as I'm a person, 'tis true! She was never
suffered to play with a male child, though but in coats; nay
her very babies were of the feminine gender. Oh, she never
looked a man in the face but her own father, or the chaplain
—and him we made a shift to put upon her for a woman, by   175
the help of his long garments and his sleek face—till she was
going in her fifteen.

MRS. MARWOOD

'Twas much she should be deceived so long.

LADY WISHFORT

I warrant you, or she would never have borne to have been
catechised by him, and have heard his long lectures against   180
singing and dancing and such debaucheries, and going to

---

160 *sha' not* Q1 (shan't Q2, Ww)
163 *stand by* Q1, Q2 (stand Ww)

---

160 *bodkin* ornamental hairpin
161 *brass counter* very small and insignificant sum of money
173 *babies* dolls
175 *made a shift to put upon her* contrived to present to her

filthy plays, and profane music-meetings, where the lewd
trebles squeak nothing but bawdy, and the basses roar blas-
phemy. Oh, she would have swooned at the sight or name of
an obscene playbook! And can I think, after all this, that my 185
daughter can be naught? What, a whore, and thought it
excommunication to set her foot within the door of a playhouse? Oh my dear friend, I can't believe it, no, no; as she
says, let him prove it, let him prove it.

MRS. MARWOOD

Prove it madam? What, and have your name prostituted in a 190
public court! Yours and your daughter's reputation worried
at the bar by a pack of bawling lawyers? To be ushered in
with an Oyez of scandal, and have your case opened by an old
fumbling lecher, in a quoif like a man midwife; to bring
your daughter's infamy to light, to be a theme for legal puns- 195
ters and quibblers by the statute, and become a jest, against a
rule of court, where there is no precedent for a jest in any
record, not even in Doomsday Book; to discompose the
gravity of the bench, and provoke naughty interrogatories in
more naughty law Latin, while the good judge, tickled with 200
the proceeding, simpers under a grey beard and fidges off
and on his cushion, as if he had swallowed cantharides,
or sat upon cow-itch.

LADY WISHFORT

Oh, 'tis very hard.

MRS. MARWOOD

And then to have my young revellers of the Temple take 205

188 *Oh my dear* Q1, Q2 (Oh dear Ww)

---

190 *Prove it.* The recital of the miseries of going to law which Mrs. Marwood
here begins owes much to the similar performance of Truewit on the
miseries of marriage in *The Silent Woman*, II, ii.

193 *Oyez* the cry 'hear ye' used by court criers to gain silence for proclama-
tions

194 *quoif* a white cap then worn by barristers

198 *Doomsday Book.* William the Conqueror's census and survey of his
new kingdom, compiled in 1085–86; proverbially used to mean 'remote
history'.

199 *naughty* lewd

201 *simpers* smirks, leers

201 *fidges* fidgets

202 *cantharides* a compound of dried beetles (Spanish Fly) thought to be
aphrodisiac because of its irritant property

203 *cow-itch* the stinging hairs of the pods of a tropical plant

205 *of the Temple* i.e. students of the Inns of Court

notes like prentices at a conventicle, and after talk it all over
again in commons, or before drawers in an eating house.

LADY WISHFORT

Worse and worse.

MRS. MARWOOD

Nay this is nothing; if it would end here, 'twere well; but it
must after this be consigned by the shorthand writers to the   210
public press, and from thence be transferred to the hands,
nay into the throats and lungs of hawkers, with voices more
licentious than the loud flounder-man's, or the woman that
cries grey peas! And this you must hear till you are stunned
—nay, you must hear nothing else for some days!   215

LADY WISHFORT

Oh, 'tis insupportable! No, no, dear friend, make it up, make
it up; ay, ay, I'll compound. I'll give up all, myself and my
all, my niece and her all—anything, everything, for composition!

MRS. MARWOOD

Nay madam, I advise nothing, I only lay before you as a   220
friend the inconveniences which perhaps you have overseen.
Here comes Mr. Fainall. If he will be satisfied to huddle up
all in silence, I shall be glad. You must think I would rather
congratulate than condole with you.

Enter FAINALL

LADY WISHFORT

Ay, ay, I do not doubt it, dear Marwood; no, no, I do not   225
doubt it.

FAINALL

Well madam, I have suffered myself to be overcome by the

---

206 *all over* Q1, Q2 (over Ww)

206 *prentices . . . conventicle.* Dissenting tradesmen customarily required
their apprentices to take notes during sermons for the later edification
of their families; the connections between Puritanism and economic
individualism in the period are discussed by Ian Watt in *The Rise of the
Novel* (London, 1952).

207 *commons* meals in hall

213 *flounder-man's.* Etherege's Harriet in *The Man of Mode*, V, ii, 433–4,
says 'There's musick in the worst Cry in *London*! *My Dill and Cow-
cumbers to pickle!*' Summers notes that a famous crier of flounders
flourished from William and Mary to the end of George I's reign and
his 'tones, in lengthening out the word flounders, were so happily
varied, that people heard him with surprise and some degree of pleasure'.

221 *overseen* overlooked

importunity of this lady your friend, and am content you
shall enjoy your own proper estate during life, on condition you oblige yourself never to marry, under such penalty   230
as I think convenient.

LADY WISHFORT

Never to marry?

FAINALL

No more Sir Rowlands; the next imposture may not be so
timely detected.

MRS. MARWOOD

That condition, I dare answer, my lady will consent to with-   235
out difficulty; she has already but too much experienced the
perfidiousness of men. Besides madam, when we retire to our
pastoral solitude we shall bid adieu to all other thoughts.

LADY WISHFORT

Ay that's true; but in case of necessity, as of health, or some
such emergency—   240

FAINALL

Oh, if you are prescribed marriage, you shall be considered; I
will only reserve to myself the power to choose for you. If
your physic be wholesome, it matters not who is your apothe-
cary. Next, my wife shall settle on me the remainder of her
fortune not made over already, and for her maintenance   245
depend entirely on my discretion.

LADY WISHFORT

This is most inhumanly savage, exceeding the barbarity
of a Muscovite husband.

FAINALL

I learned it from his Czarish majesty's retinue, in a winter
evening's conference over brandy and pepper, amongst   250
other secrets of matrimony and policy, as they are at present

248 *Muscovite husband.* Peter the Great visited London in 1697, which
perhaps refreshed English attitudes to Russian matrimonial customs,
formed by Elizabethan travellers' accounts. Anthony Jenkinson, for
instance, in 1558, wrote: 'When they are going to bedde, the bridegrome
putteth certain money, both golde and silver, if he have it, into one of his
boots and then sitteth down in the chamber, crossing his legges, and
then the bride must plucke off one of his boots . . . if she misse the
boot wherein the money is, she doth not only loose the money, but is
also bound from that day forwards to pull of his boots continually . . .
one common rule is amongst them, if the woman be not beaten with the
whip once a weeke, she will not be good, and therefore they looke for it
orderly, & the women say, that if their husbands did not beate them,
they should not love them.' (*Hakluyt's Voyages[* Glasgow, 1903], II,
446).

practised in the northern hemisphere. But this must be
agreed unto, and that positively. Lastly, I will be endowed in
right of my wife with that six thousand pound which is the
moiety of Mrs. Millamant's fortune in your possession, and   255
which she has forfeited (as will appear by the last will and
testament of your deceased husband Sir Jonathan Wishfort)
by her disobedience in contracting herself against your
consent or knowledge, and by refusing the offered match
with Sir Wilfull Witwoud, which you, like a careful aunt,   260
had provided for her.

LADY WISHFORT

My nephew was *non compos*, and could not make his
addresses.

FAINALL

I come to make demands—I'll hear no objections.

LADY WISHFORT

You will grant me time to consider.   265

FAINALL

Yes, while the instrument is drawing to which you must set
your hand, till more sufficient deeds can be perfected;
which I will take care shall be done with all possible speed.
In the mean while, I will go for the said instrument, and
till my return you may balance this matter in your own   270
discretion.   *Exit* FAINALL

LADY WISHFORT

This insolence is beyond all precedent, all parallel! Must
I be subject to this merciless villain?

MRS. MARWOOD

'Tis severe indeed, madam, that you should smart for your
daughter's wantonness.   275

LADY WISHFORT

'Twas against my consent that she married this barbarian,
but she would have him, though her year was not out. Ah,
her first husband, my son Languish, would not have carried
it thus. Well, that was my choice, this is hers; she is matched
now with a witness! I shall be mad, dear friend, is there no   280
comfort for me? Must I live to be confiscated at this rebel
rate? Here come two more of my Egyptian plagues, too.

262 *non compos* not in his right mind
266 *instrument* document
277 *her year* her year's mourning for her first husband
280 *with a witness* emphatic phrase, equivalent to 'with a vengeance' (Lynch)
281 *rebel* extortionate
282 *Egyptian plagues* see Exodus 7–12. Ten plagues visited the Pharaoh.

Enter MILLAMANT *and* SIR WILFULL

SIR WILFULL
Aunt, your servant.
LADY WISHFORT
Out, caterpillar, call not me aunt, I know thee not.
SIR WILFULL
I confess I have been a little in disguise as they say; 'sheart,   285
and I'm sorry for't. What would you have? I hope I com-
mitted no offence, aunt, and if I did I am willing to make
satisfaction: and what can a man say fairer? If I have broke
anything, I'll pay for't, an it cost a pound; and so let that
content for what's past, and make no more words. For   290
what's to come, to pleasure you I'm willing to marry my
cousin; so pray let's all be friends. She and I are agreed
upon the matter, before a witness.
LADY WISHFORT
How's this, dear niece? Have I any comfort? Can this be
true?   295
MILLAMANT
I am content to be a sacrifice to your repose, madam; and to
convince you that I had no hand in the plot, as you were mis-
informed, I have laid my commands on Mirabell to come in
person and be a witness that I give my hand to this flower of
knighthood; and, for the contract that passed between   300
Mirabell and me, I have obliged him to make a resignation
of it in your ladyship's presence. He is without and waits
your leave for admittance.
LADY WISHFORT
Well, I'll swear I am something revived at this testimony of
your obedience, but I cannot admit that traitor—I fear I can-   305
not fortify myself to support his appearance. He is as terrible
to me as a Gorgon; if I see him, I fear I shall turn to stone,
petrify incessantly.
MILLAMANT
If you disoblige him he may resent your refusal and insist
upon the contract still; then 'tis the last time he will be   310
offensive to you.
LADY WISHFORT
Are you sure it will be the last time? If I were sure of that—
shall I never see him again?

285 *in disguise* intoxicated
307 *Gorgon* three mythical ladies with snakes instead of hair whose look had
the power to petrify. Perseus slew one of them, Medusa.

MILLAMANT

Sir Wilfull, you and he are to travel together, are you not?

SIR WILFULL

'Sheart, the gentleman's a civil gentleman, aunt, let him   315
come in. Why, we are sworn brothers and fellow travellers.
We are to be Pylades and Orestes, he and I; he is to be my
interpreter in foreign parts. He has been overseas once
already; and with proviso, that I marry my cousin, will cross
'em once again, only to bear me company. 'Sheart, I'll call   320
him in. An I set on't once, he shall come in—and see
who'll hinder him!   *Exit*

MRS. MARWOOD

This is precious fooling, if it would pass, but I'll know the
bottom of it.

LADY WISHFORT

Oh dear Marwood, you are not going?   325

MRS. MARWOOD

Not far, madam; I'll return immediately.   *Exit*

Enter SIR WILFULL *and* MIRABELL

SIR WILFULL

Look up man, I'll stand by you; 'sbud, an she do frown, she
can't kill you! Besides—harkee—she dare not frown des-
perately, because her face is none of her own. 'Sheart, an she
should, her forehead would wrinkle like the coat of a cream   330
cheese; but mum for that, fellow traveller.

MIRABELL

If a deep sense of the many injuries I have offered to so good
a lady, with a sincere remorse, and a hearty contrition, can
but obtain the least glance of compassion, I am too happy.
Ah madam, there was a time—but let it be forgotten—I   335
confess I have deservedly forefeited the high place I once
held, of sighing at your feet. Nay, kill me not by turning from
me in disdain—I come not to plead for favour, nay, not for
pardon—I am a suppliant only for your pity. I am going
where I never shall behold you more—   340

---

327 *an she* Q1 (and she Q2, Ww)
339 *for your pity* Q1, Q2 (for pity Ww)

---

317 *Pylades and Orestes* famous friends and travelling companions in
    Greek myth and in the dramatisation of the Orestes story by Aeschylus
330–1 *coat of a cream cheese* a fine image, perhaps suggested by Jonson,
    Every Man Out Of His Humour, I, ii, 58–9: 'looke with a good startch't
    face, and ruffle your brow like a new boot'

SIR WILFULL

How, fellow traveller? You shall go by yourself then!

MIRABELL

Let me be pitied first, and afterwards forgotten. I ask no more.

SIR WILFULL

By'r Lady, a very reasonable request, and will cost you nothing, aunt. Come, come, forgive and forget, aunt. Why, 345 you must an you are a Christian.

MIRABELL

Consider, madam, in reality, you could not receive much prejudice. It was an innocent device, though I confess it had a face of guiltiness. It was at most an artifice which love contrived, and errors which love produces have ever been 350 accounted venial. At least think it is punishment enough that I have lost what in my heart I hold most dear; that to your cruel indignation I have offered up this beauty, and with her my peace and quiet, nay, all my hopes of future comfort. 355

SIR WILFUL

An he does not move me, would I might never be o' the Quorum! An it were not as good a deed as to drink, to give her to him again, I would I might never take shipping! Aunt, if you don't forgive quickly, I shall melt, I can tell you that. My contract went no further than a little mouth-glue, and 360 that's hardly dry; one doleful sigh more from my fellow traveller, and 'tis dissolved.

LADY WISHFORT

Well, nephew, upon your account—ah, he has a false insinuating tongue—well sir, I will stifle my just resentment at my nephew's request, I will endeavour what I can to for- 365 get, but on proviso that you resign the contract with my niece immediately.

MIRABELL

It is in writing and with papers of concern, but I have sent my servant for it, and will deliver it to you with all acknow- ledgements for your transcendent goodness. 370

LADY WISHFORT (*Aside*)

Oh he has witchcraft in his eyes and tongue! When I did not

---

356 *would I might* Q1, Q2 (would I may Ww)

---

357 *Quorum.* To be 'of the Quorum' meant to be a Justice of the Peace.
360 *mouth-glue.* It was only an oral promise.

see him I could have bribed a villain to his assassination; but his appearance rakes the embers which have so long lain smothered in my breast.

Enter FAINALL *and* MRS. MARWOOD

FAINALL

Your date of deliberation, madam, is expired. Here is the   375
instrument; are you prepared to sign?

LADY WISHFORT

If I were prepared, I am not empowered. My niece exerts a lawful claim, having matched herself by my direction to Sir Wilfull.

FAINALL

That sham is too gross to pass on me, though 'tis imposed on   380
you, madam.

MILLAMANT

Sir, I have given my consent.

MIRABELL

And sir, I have resigned my pretensions.

SIR WILFULL

And sir, I assert my right, and will maintain it in defiance of you, sir, and of your instrument. 'Sheart, an you talk of an   385
instrument, sir, I have an old fox by my thigh shall hack your instrument of ram vellum to shreds, sir! It shall not be sufficient for a *mittimus* or a tailor's measure! Therefore withdraw your instrument sir, or by'r Lady I shall draw mine.   390

LADY WISHFORT

Hold, nephew, hold.

MILLAMANT

Good Sir Wilfull, respite your valour.

FAINALL

Indeed, are you provided of a guard, with your single Beefeater there? But I'm prepared for you, and insist upon my first proposal. You shall submit your own estate to my   395

393 *a guard* Q1 (your guard Q2, Ww)

---

386 *fox* sword

387 *ram vellum* parchment made from sheepskin

388 *mittimus* order to the keeper of a prison to receive and keep the individual specified in the warrant

388 *tailor's measure* a parchment strip, like a modern tape measure, with measurements marked along it

394 *Beefeater* a yeoman of the guard, proverbial for bulk and strength; also used insultingly to mean 'fat menial'

management, and absolutely make over my wife's to my sole
use, as pursuant to the purport and tenor of this other
covenant. I suppose madam [*to* MILLAMANT] your consent is
not requisite in this case, nor, Mr. Mirabell, your resignation, nor, Sir Wilfull, your right. You may draw your fox   400
if you please, sir, and make a bear-garden flourish somewhere else—for here it will not avail. This, my Lady
Wishfort, must be subscribed, or your darling daughter's
turned adrift like a leaky hulk to sink or swim, as she and
the current of this lewd town can agree.   405

LADY WISHFORT

Is there no means, no remedy, to stop my ruin? Ungrateful
wretch! Dost thou not owe thy being, thy subsistence, to my
daughter's fortune?

FAINALL

I'll answer you when I have the rest of it in my possession.

MIRABELL

But that you would not accept of a remedy from my hands—   410
I own I have not deserved you should owe any obligation to
me, or else, perhaps, I could advise—

LADY WISHFORT

Oh what, what? To save me and my child from ruin, from
want, I'll forgive all that's past, nay, I'll consent to anything
to come, to be delivered from this tyranny.   415

MIRABELL

Ay madam, but that is too late; my reward is intercepted;
you have disposed of her who only could have made me a
compensation for all my services—but be it as it may. I am
resolved I'll serve you, you shall not be wronged in this
savage manner.   420

LADY WISHFORT

How! Dear Mr. Mirabell, can you be so generous at last?
But it is not possible. Harkee, I'll break my nephew's match,
you shall have my niece yet and all her fortune, if you can but
save me from this imminent danger.

MIRABELL

Will you? I take you at your word. I ask no more. I must have 425
leave for two criminals to appear.

LADY WISHFORT

Ay, ay, anybody, anybody.

401 *bear-garden flourish* behaviour suited to the gross and crudely violent
atmosphere in which bear-baitings took place; with a subsidiary allusion to the old-fashioned, Elizabethan impulse of Sir Wilfull to use his
sword

MIRABELL

Foible is one, and a penitent.

Enter MRS. FAINALL, FOIBLE, *and* MINCING

MRS. MARWOOD (*to* FAINALL)

Oh my shame! These corrupt things are bought and brought
hither to expose me.   430

MIRABELL *and* LADY WISHFORT *go to* MRS. FAINALL *and* FOIBLE

FAINALL

If it must all come out, why, let 'em know it, 'tis but the way
of the world. That shall not urge me to relinquish or abate
one tittle of my terms, no, I will insist the more.

FOIBLE

Yes indeed madam, I'll take my Bible oath of it.

MINCING

And so will I, mem.   435

LADY WISHFORT

Oh Marwood, Marwood, art thou false? My friend deceive
me? Hast thou been a wicked accomplice with that profligate
man?

MRS. MARWOOD

Have you so much ingratitude and injustice to give credit
against your friend to the aspersions of two such mercenary   440
trulls?

MINCING

Mercenary mem? I scorn your words. 'Tis true we found you
and Mr. Fainall in the blue garret; by the same token, you
swore us to secrecy upon Messalina's poems. Mercenary?
No, if we would have been mercenary we should have held   445
our tongues; you would have bribed us sufficiently.

FAINALL

Go, you are an insignificant thing. Well, what are you the
better for this? Is this Mr. Mirabell's expedient? I'll be put
off no longer. You thing that was a wife shall smart for this—
I will not leave thee wherewithal to hide thy shame. Your   450
body shall be naked as your reputation.

---

429 *bought and brought* Q1, Q2 (brought Ww)

---

444 *Messalina.* The notoriously licentious wife of the Roman emperor
Claudius could have inspired a collection of obscene poems, though
there is no record of one at the time; but Mincing may be mispronounc-
ing 'Miscellany'.

MRS. FAINALL

I despise you and defy your malice. You have aspersed me
wrongfully; I have proved your falsehood. Go, you and your
treacherous—I will not name it—but starve together,
perish!   455

FAINALL

Not while you are worth a groat! Indeed, my dear madam,
I'll be fooled no longer.

LADY WISHFORT

Ah Mr. Mirabell, this is small comfort, the detection of this
affair.

MIRABELL

Oh in good time; your leave for the other offender and   460
penitent to appear, madam.

Enter WAITWELL *with a box of writings*

LADY WISHFORT

Oh, Sir Rowland! Well, rascal?

WAITWELL

What your ladyship pleases. I have brought the black box
at last, madam.

MIRABELL

Give it me. Madam, you remember your promise?   465

LADY WISHFORT

Ay, dear sir.

MIRABELL

Where are the gentlemen?

WAITWELL

At hand sir, rubbing their eyes—just risen from sleep.

FAINALL

'Sdeath what's this to me? I'll not wait your private concerns.

Enter PETULANT *and* WITWOUD

PETULANT

How now, what's the matter? Whose hand's out?   470

WITWOUD

Heyday! What, are you all got together like players at the
end of the last act?

MIRABELL

You may remember gentlemen, I once requested your hands
as witnesses to a certain parchment.

456 *groat* coin of derisory low value
470 *Whose hand's out* reminiscent of *2 Henry IV*, II, i, 40–41, when Falstaff
    exclaims 'How now! Whose mare's dead? What's the matter?'

WITWOUD

Ay, I do, my hand, I remember—Petulant set his mark.   475

MIRABELL

You wrong him, his name is fairly written, as shall appear.
You do not remember, gentlemen, anything of what that
parchment contained?

                                        (*undoing the box*)

WITWOUD

No.

PETULANT

Not I. I writ. I read nothing.   480

MIRABELL

Very well, now you shall know. Madam, your promise.

LADY WISHFORT

Ay, ay, sir, upon my honour.

MIRABELL

Mr. Fainall, it is now time that you should know that your
lady, while she was at her own disposal, and before you had
by your insinuations wheedled her out of a pretended settle-   485
ment of the greatest part of her fortune—

FAINALL

Sir! Pretended!

MIRABELL

Yes sir. I say that this lady, while a widow, having it seems
received some cautions respecting your inconstancy and
tyranny of temper, which from her own partial opinion   490
and fondness of you she could never have suspected—she
did, I say, by the wholesome advice of friends and of sages
learned in the laws of this land, deliver this same as her act
and deed to me in trust, and to the uses within mentioned.
You may read if you please, (*holding out the parchment*)   495
though perhaps what is inscribed on the back may serve your
occasions.

FAINALL

Very likely, sir. What's here? Damnation! (*reads*) 'A deed of
conveyance of the whole estate real of Arabella Languish
widow, in trust to Edward Mirabell'. Confusion!   500

MIRABELL

Even so sir, 'tis the way of the world, sir, of the widows of the
world. I suppose this deed may bear an elder date than what
you have obtained from your lady.

496 *inscribed* Q1, Q2 (written Ww)

499 *conveyance* the written instrument for legal transference of real property

FAINALL

Perfidious fiend! Then thus I'll be revenged!
Offers to run at MRS. FAINALL

SIR WILFULL

Hold sir, now you may make your bear-garden flourish   505
somewhere else, sir.

FAINALL

Mirabell, you shall hear of this, sir, be sure you shall: let me
pass, oaf!   *Exit*

MRS. FAINALL

Madam, you seem to stifle your resentment; you had better
give it vent.   510

MRS. MARWOOD

Yes it shall have vent, and to your confusion, or I'll perish in
the attempt.   *Exit*

LADY WISHFORT

Oh daughter, daughter, 'tis plain thou hast inherited thy
mother's prudence.

MRS. FAINALL

Thank Mr. Mirabell, a cautious friend, to whose advice all is   515
owing.

LADY WISHFORT

Well Mr. Mirabell, you have kept your promise, and I must
perform mine. First I pardon for your sake Sir Rowland
there, and Foible; the next thing is to break the matter to my
nephew—and how to do that—   520

MIRABELL

For that, madam, give yourself no trouble, let me have your
consent. Sir Wilfull is my friend, he has had compassion
upon lovers and generously engaged a volunteer in this
action, for our service, and now designs to prosecute his
travels.   525

SIR WILFULL

'Sheart aunt I have no mind to marry. My cousin's a fine lady,
and the gentleman loves her and she loves him, and they
deserve one another. My resolution is to see foreign parts—I
have set on't—and when I'm set on't, I must do't—and
if these two gentlemen would travel too, I think they may be   530
spared.

PETULANT

For my part, I say little; I think things are best off or on.

WITWOUD

Egad I understand nothing of the matter; I'm in a maze yet,
like a dog in a dancing school.

LADY WISHFORT

Well sir, take her, and with her all the joy I can give you.   535

MILLAMANT

Why does not the man take me? Would you have me give
myself to you over again?

MIRABELL

Ay, and over and over again, for (*kisses her hand*) I would have
you as often as possibly I can. Well, heaven grant I love you
not too well, that's all my fear.   540

SIR WILFULL

'Sheart you'll have time enough to toy after you're married;
or, if you will toy now, let us have a dance in the mean time,
that we, who are not lovers, may have some other employ-
ment besides looking on.

MIRABELL

With all my heart, dear Sir Wilfull; what shall we do for   545
music?

FOIBLE

Oh sir, some that were provided for Sir Rowland's entertainment are yet within call.

A dance

LADY WISHFORT

As I am a person I can hold out no longer. I have wasted
my spirits so today already, that I am ready to sink under the   550
fatigue; and I cannot but have some fears upon me yet that
my son Fainall will pursue some desperate course.

MIRABELL

Madam, disquiet not yourself on that account; to my
knowledge his circumstances are such, he must of force
comply. For my part I will contribute all that in me lies   555
to a reunion. In the mean time, madam (*to* MRS. FAINALL)
let me, before these witnesses, restore to you this deed of
trust. It may be a means, well managed, to make you live
easily together.

From hence let those be warned, who mean to wed,   560
Lest mutual falsehood stain the bridal bed;
For each deceiver to his cost may find
That marriage frauds, too oft, are paid in kind. *Exeunt*

538 *for* (omitted Q2, Ww)
541 *have time enough* ed. (have him time enough Q1, Q2)

541 *toy* embrace

EPILOGUE
Spoken by Mrs. Bracegirdle

After our Epilogue this crowd dismisses,
I'm thinking how this play'll be pulled to pieces.
But pray consider, ere you doom its fall,
How hard a thing 'twould be to please you all.
There are some critics so with spleen diseased   5
They scarcely come inclining to be pleased;
And sure he must have more than mortal skill
Who pleases anyone against his will.
Then, all bad poets, we are sure, are foes,
And how their number's swelled, the town well knows.   10
In shoals I've marked 'em judging in the pit,
Though they're on no pretence for judgement fit,
But that they have been damned, for want of wit.
Since when they, by their own offences taught,
Set up for spies on plays, and finding fault.   15
Others there are whose malice we'd prevent;
Such who watch plays with scurrilous intent
To mark out who by characters are meant,
And though no perfect likeness they can trace
Yet each pretends to know the copied face.   20
These with false glosses feed their own ill nature,
And turn to libel, what was meant a satire.
May such malicious fops this fortune find,
To think themselves alone the fools designed,
If any are so arrogantly vain   25
To think they singly can support a scene
And furnish fool enough to entertain.
For well the learned and the judicious know
That satire scorns to stoop so meanly low,
As any one abstracted fop to show.   30
For as when painters form a matchless face
They, from each fair one, catch some different grace,

2 *I'm* ed. (In Q1)

---

21 *glosses* explanatory notes
30 *abstracted* specially chosen from his fellows

115

And shining features in one portrait blend,
To which no single beauty must pretend;
So poets oft do in one piece expose   35
Whole *belles assemblées* of coquettes and beaux.

FINIS